YOU WANT IT?
YOU'LL MAKE IT!

I dedicate this book to all those

who have supported me in my sporting career:

the promoters of my various projects,

my sponsors, backers and

especially my wife Doris,

without whose generous support

many of my accomplishments

would never have come to pass.

YOU WANT IT?
YOU'LL MAKE IT!

3nd. Edition 2013

Colorama Verlagsgesellschaft mbH
A-5020 Salzburg
www.colorama.at

ISBN: 978-3-901988-93-6

Layout, print and typography
Colordruck GmbH
Kalkofenweg 6, A-5400 Hallein
www.colordruck.at

Coverdesign: Reichl und Partner

Cover photo: Heiko Mandl

Photos: Dmitry Pichugin – Fotolia.com
Wolfgang Luef, Alois Furtner,
Privat archive Wolfgang Fasching

Overall design: Doris Fasching, Günter Weixlbaumer

FOREWORD

In the case of Wolfgang Fasching's book, the term Foreword can best be taken literally. Only one word does it justice: "Stupendous"! Since what this man has undertaken, put into action and finally achieved over his sporting career is truly stupendous. Stupendous – not easy for an average chap like me to understand. I couldn't imagine myself biking all over the USA, exhausted through lack of sleep and going at one heck of a pace.

The book's title says it all: "You want it? You'll make it! ". To be sure, you have to have the talent and flair for any job – but ambition and motivation are no less important. I, for my part, wanted to be a successful professional footballer. On the way I encountered no end of obstacles, one of which was my former trainer Erich Hof, who had high hopes of everything – except me. But these stumbling blocks can be overcome so long as you have faith in yourself and your objectives.

I proved this in 1993 when I moved from the Spanish league to FC Cologne. This change was accompanied by incredible problems with the media. German newspapers screamed: Why do you want a slow, cumbersome Austrian? The media put a negative spin on the many advance plaudits. I just had to prove my worth – and went out and did it! No-one believed in me: "He'll never pull it off!" They said. But I did pull it off. In the 1996/97 season I was the second highest German goal scorer!

In his book, Wolfgang Fasching not only sketches out his life but also gives valuable tips. It should not only be a ready standby for every dedicated sports(wo)man, but also be avidly read by the ordinary man-in-the-street or stressed managers since Fasching gives practical tips for "everyday" life also.

Wolfgang Fasching being a man of extremes, his book is extremely important and of the highest quality. Hopefully not his last.

TONI POLSTER

INTRODUCTION

When professional cyclists ended their training after 180 kilometers and returned home, I felt that the fun only just started, and I did a few extra rounds. In 1988, when I watched an impressive documentary about the Race Across America on TV, a thought settled in my head: this is a race I want to do! The Race Across America is a cycle race that leads nonstop through the United States. Approx. 5,000 kilometers have to be covered, with 30,000 metres altitude difference. In addition, one has to cope with extreme differences in temperature: between pleasant 25 degrees on the west coast, extreme 50 degrees in the Utah desert, and moderate 0 degrees in the Rocky Mountains. The athletes burn up to 20,000 calories a day, have to drink approx. 25 litres and have to contend themselves with not more than 10 hours of sleep per week. However, the one who wants to be up ahead has to get by on less than 10 hours of sleep in the course of the eight or nine days that it takes on the bike from the west coast to the east coast of the USA. And exactly this race with such seemingly impossible benchmark data turned out to be "my" destiny. Eight times I participated in the Race Across America, and each time I stood on the podium, three times at the very top. In 2001, I was the 13th Austrian on top of Mount Everest, I was 24-hour World and European Champion, world record holder on the long distance, and I was victorious in various extreme cycle races.

One thing has always particularly motivated me: the more intensively I engaged in a project, the stronger was the will to see it through. Following the motto: "You want it? You'll make it!" Since I attend the College for Mental Training in Bregenz, I become more and more aware that I have, in my life as an extreme athlete, automatically applied many of the theories that are taught there. At the time, I applied those theories without knowing the various techniques and methods.

My childhood was tough. I was born on August 11, 1967, as the youngest child of four in Bad Radkersburg in Styria. My early childhood was not easy, my parents' marriage was shattered. My father became more and more depressed after a caterpillar accident and started drinking. We dealt with divorce, the Welfare Centre, financial difficulties. Life gave 6 year old Wolfgang no quarter. My mother brought us children up without a husband, luxury was unknown. She was a fighter and accomplished heroic deeds – she never let us children down. Then, my 10 year old brother Walter fell ill with cancer. Fate was not on our side. After ten years and countless operations, Walter beat the cancer. Our youth shaped our future lives as well: we learned to never give up. Stamina and endurance were drummed into us in our earliest childhood!

At school, I was a mediocre student. For me, sports and exercise were a chance to escape from the daily routine. I competed in my first cycle race at the age of 12 in my hometown of Straden, using a miserable bicycle. It was an unlicensed race, and I ended up in 7th place. My second experience with cycle racing happened not long afterwards. The stars of the Austrian cycling scene gave a guest performance in Straden. In pouring rain, I was inspired by the sportsmen and collected autographs from the athletes, attendants and engineers. These people fascinated me, although I preferred to spend my time on the pitch; at the time, I was goalkeeper with my hometown soccer club. After compulsory school, I completed an apprenticeship as a painter. Cycling as a sport hardly played a role until my first year as an apprentice. And then, when I earned scant 100 Euro per month, my love for cycling flared up. I decided to buy myself a bike, a Puch Clubmann, which cost 200 Euro. I made a down payment of 50 and paid off the rest in monthly installments. After 3 years as a painter's apprentice and after obtaining my trade test degree, I joined the army and bound myself as a regular soldier for 4 years.

If you have exceptional visions and ideas in your head,
only tell others about them
when you can actually realize your ideas!

When I was 18, I watched Franz Spilauer, who was the first European to win the Race Across America, in a sports documentary on TV. The report, which showed a lone fighter in San

Francisco, city of dreams, with its steep streets and the endless vastness of America, was accompanied by the song "San Francisco Bay". All this fascinated me, and I could not get it out of my head. And this was although my interest was more inclined to soccer then. My experience with cycling was confined to the daily 32 kilometers I had to cover every day between my home and my workplace when I was an apprentice. The very next day after that TV documentary, I went to my mother and told her proudly what it was I meant to do. Full of enthusiasm, I told her the story of an Austrian who had won the Race Across America. With all the benchmark data and my intention to participate myself. She countered as was to be expected from a mother, "Wolfgang, you don't know anybody there, the country is unknown to you, and your English isn't good enough. And what's more, you're not such a good cyclist! And how do you want to finance such a thing? You don't have any money. And on top, it is dangerous!" She had a lot of watertight arguments to dissuade me. I thought, "Yes, she's right. It's nonsense." But two days later, at the back of my head, the thought took hold once more. The fascination of the Race Across America would not let me go again. I had learned my first big lesson: If you have exceptional visions and ideas in your head, only tell others about them when you can actually realize your ideas. You will have a lot of people around you (friends, relatives, colleagues) who will nip your ideas in the bud: Why you of all people are not going to make it! Sometimes, they argue against it, because they mean "well" with you. Often, envy plays a role. I took my experience to heart that day and decided to keep my future visions to myself until I could actually realize them. So as not to topple down prematurely under arguments next time.

In the years to come, I could not get the vision of starting at the Race Across America out of my head. Still, my life took its normal course, though it wasn't all that normal, admittedly: The 3 years of my apprenticeship to a painter had to be. My mother insisted, because I needed a proper job. I served my time for the necessary 3 years exactly, not one day longer. Then I spent four years in the army. Although many people have a low opinion of the army, I managed to come away with a few positive aspects for my future: punctuality, discipline and order, all things you need in life, and the more so in sports. Afterwards, aged 22, I started another apprenticeship, this time as a retailer. This career led to my being an independent tradesman for 9 years. Alongside this, I went to evening classes for 3 years to get a non-academic degree for retail marketing. My career as a cyclist went its course with unhindered consequence. When I was 25, my daughter Simone was born. The day only had 24 hours then as it has now, a few too few. During my first phase as an endurance athlete, many people declared me completely crazy. But I was exceedingly ambitious and diligent. I got up at 5 o'clock every morning and exercised for my project, the Race Across America. Often, I did my exercises feeling a touch of bad conscience, because I thought I was letting down my employees in the shop. What will they think of me? The boss is going cycling, and his staff is working day and night? But I managed to balance everything. Get up at 5 am, exercise, go to work, then go cycling again, back to work, until late at night. Three to four times a week, I went to Graz, 70 km away, and back home, to attend evening classes. Many people thought I had better use my energy for my work. Sports don't pay. He doesn't earn anything with this! But I was adamant, always convinced of my goal and success.

At that time, I cycled for the local cycling club. It was there I met Peter Luttenberger, the winner of the Tour de Suisse and fifth in the Tour de France in 1996. He only lived 15 km away, and we exercised together almost every day. Lightweight Peter got ahead fast both at home and abroad. Due to my multiple loads (family, work, sports and studies), I was not able to live 100% for cycling, like he could.

Sports and exercise were my life. After my exercise periods, I devoured the sports pages of the newspapers and dug through all the sports magazines. Sportsmen have always been role models for me, and I've always wanted to be one of those people looking at you from a newspaper. This dream, which I had already had as a child, I wanted to achieve. I started in the class of the hobby cyclists. Insecurity and fright prevented me from winning in the first real race. I simply did not know what to do on reaching the finish line being first. Even though it would only have been a triumph in the hobby class – I was first, close to the finish, looked back, and the distance would have been big enough. I slowed down, hesitated, and it did not take long until a rival overtook me. I never was the type to cross the finish line arms stretched wide, I never did this, not even at the end of my career. I hardly ever displayed my emotions. I finished my "premiere race" in third place. But I had my first victory with the very next race, and I pocketed the necessary successes very fast, so I could enter the next level, the class of the main cyclists.

It often happens after races that I go home not in the team coach but on my bike. Long races and adverse atmospheric conditions are congenial to me. The persevering streak was in me. As was the vision of the Race Across America and the vision to always do more than the others! I cannot say why this was and is so. I suppose it is because of my socially impaired background. My father had left us at an early stage, he did not treat his wife and us children well. The people in the village could often be heard saying, "The children will take after the father." I always knew then: I do not want to be like him! So there never was a danger of my degenerating into a ruffian or a drunkard. This was a clear resolution, almost like an auto-suggestion.

My interest in classic cycling races waned more and more. I decided to focus on long distance races and participated in the first 12 and 24 hour races. The vision of the Race Across America became increasingly manifest and culminated in May 1995 in the actual realization: I participated in the official qualifying race to the RAAM. The route was from Bregenz to Vienna, covering 800 kilometres. With second place and only 3 minutes behind the German world class triathlete Lothar Leder I managed the first hurdle! The door to America was open wide. All I had to do was pass through! Which meant: find sponsors, put together a team and start intensive preparations for the classic in America!

I was so happy and proud, and at the same time nervous and excited as never before, when on August 1st, 1996, I got out of bed at 6 o'clock in the morning in Irvine, the starting place of the Race Across America. At breakfast, I couldn't eat a thing. The last preparations until the presentation of the cyclists at 8:30 lasted forever. Then we were presented individually by the moderator, first the rookies, and the stars last. I was lucky in that a TV team was also there. I still remember a remark of the editorial journalist: "If you make it to halftime, we can make something of it." I was shocked! For me it had always been clear that I would see this through. There was nothing that could have kept me from it. My sponsors, for whom such an engagement was something completely new, had also asked, "What happens if you drop out?" Such questions I left unanswered, there never was the slightest doubt from my side. Once I start something, I finish it. Imminent to the start, my pulse went up to 120 beats per minute. I did not even know whether I would manage to get moving at all, that's how nervous I was. The challenge was enormous, one of the biggest in my life. My greatest worry was the great heat of up to 45 degrees Celsius right after the start. I started talking to myself, "Ride slowly, you're doing fine." The Americans were amazed, there is an Austrian there who rides ahead, he'll be in for a surprise. Suddenly I reached the finish in third place, that was a rookie record. After 8 days and 14 hours, I reached the finish. For the last 30 years of Race Across America, no rookie had managed to get through his first race in less than nine days.

The first thought at the finish was, "I have reached what I had been working for for 10 years. Never again!" But on the way home to Austria, I was already planning my next Race Across America. There was only one big difference: I knew that I was able to win that race. Back home, a few days later in August, I attended a party in my honour. Contact to newspapers, lots of people that lined the street and cheered – and the critics shouted, "I've always known that the boy will make it!"

I never let any doubt arise I would not make it.

I never let any doubt arise that I would not make it. My highest goal has always been: get there. What you think will happen, what you fear will happen, and what you wish will also happen. Outwards, I always said I wanted to get through, into the top five. It was always clear to myself that I wanted to stand on the podium. And where did I finish? Third place. I had images in my head at my first arrival at the finish. My will was so strong, this was enough.

I have always known where I came from, where I belong. Due to this, I never had problems adjusting between the vastness of the RAAM and my life at home. Never to lift off, always to keep down to reality, this has always been my creed. Especially in a race like the Race Across America, where I was lucky to experience so many moments of bliss. There were a lot of such moments, but there also were tough times. After all, there is a separate story behind every race. The first one I finished third, a sensation. The second one I won. Incredible – a dream came true! I thought, "When you win the second race, you have to do it again, this is logical, isn't it?" Next time, I was far behind after the first third, last place, fighting with the cooling period. And then I broke my collarbone and was second, nevertheless. For the Americans, this was a top story! This guy crashes, breaks his collarbone, and finishes the race, pure dramaturgy! Then I participated once again. The next story: At the finish, I was less than an hour behind the winner. Over a distance of 5,000 kilometres, this is crazy! So increase the risk next time, this paid off: I won with a record winning margin of 23 hours. There had never been anything like it in the history of the RAAM. Two years later the third and thus historic triumph. Apart from Rob Kish and myself, no athlete had ever managed three victories before! Another two years later the next third place, and 2007, at the end of my career, the glamorous punch line with second place. The 8th time on the podium. This is also a record!

„You want it? You'll make it!"

„You want it? You'll make it!" is a seemingly simple sentence with a lot of potential. A potential I want to explain in this book. I am writing here about my personal experiences and practice I gained during my life as an extreme athlete, a family man and entrepreneur. My basic message is: nothing works by itself, everybody has to contribute his/her share. Every one of us needs goals that are realistic and achievable, and those goals have to be followed continuously and consistently. One of the prime examples of consistency come alive for me is one of the best known Austrians of all times. He was asked about his factors of success. His reply was:

Visions
Consistency and hard work
positive frame of mind and enthusiasm

These words are by Arnold Schwarzenegger. The born Styrian really had visions and never lost sight of his goals: at the age of 20 he was proclaimed Mister Universe, at the age of 40 he was the highest paid Hollywood star, shortly before reaching the age of 60 he was elected governor of California. There is only one last logical step on his way up: at the age of 80 at the latest, he will be the President of the United States of America.

Successful people don't just fall from the sky. There is no classification of successful and unsuccessful. Everybody has to work for his/her own success, sometimes one has to fight for it. Often, one has to face destitution. Time and time again, especially after extreme cycle races with thousands of kilometers and a minimum of sleep, I was confronted with catchwords like "inhuman, abnormal, incredible, extreme".

To me, however, my 8 participations in the Race Across America and crossing Australia, climbing Mount Everest, all this wasn't a superhuman or extraterrestrial thing to do. In my life, I have covered 650,000 kilometres on the bike, this is equivalent to 15 times round the Earth. My profession as athlete is now history, and I have always seen it as something normal. In any case more normal than sitting behind a desk for 8 hours a day.

As a competitive athlete, you have to be 100% fit to have absolute success. But as the saying goes, it's all in the head! Like when somebody is asleep at the switch or a misplayed penalty is due to nervousness. This book will help you make use of your subconscious. The precise area which controls our bodily functions, our thinking, our habits, our life. We still are not capable of using the biggest part of our brain!

When I am asked for my rules of success, my answers correspond to those of my fellow country man Arnold Schwarzenegger. I do, however, add an important point: develop enthusiasm and a passion for your vision. And the path to your goal will be much more enjoyable for you.

With this, I have reached the title of my book again: "You want it? You'll make it!" is all in the head, is all about our images, thoughts, dreams, goals, and about the unused possibilities in the mental field. Each of us wants to become more successful and lead a happy life. However, it won't be enough to aspire to your goals. You also have to live them! Like a professional athlete who lives for his/her sport 24 hours a day. Start now!

Can you feel your goal?
Do you get goose bumps when you think of it?

VISIONS AND GOALS

When I started with cycling and for the first time watched the endurance athlete Franz Spilauer on TV at the Race Across America, I was fascinated! Fascinated by the inhuman performance, the emotions, the adventure, the drama of the race! The vision of the RAAM fixed itself in my head and never let go all through the following years. It was my goal to stand on the starting line there at least once. With all the things around it, the attendants, the media. I started to train, gave cycling the topmost priority, entered competitions, and soon success proved me right. From head to toe, I was focused on the Race Across America and the further projects that followed. I had shivers from my toes up to the tips of my hair when I simply thought about the RAAM. The truth is, I only wanted to compete once, but in the course of my career, it eventually came down to eight participations. And year after year, I motivated myself anew, trained harder and more professionally for the year to come. In 2007, my career finally approached its close. For years on end, my whole life, my daily routine was subordinated to sports, training and deprivation. On June 18, when, in my last Race Across America, I passed the finishing line in second place, I ended my active career after careful considerations. In the true sense of the word, I chucked in my bike. As far as cycling was concerned, where I could realize all my dreams, I was missing the goals and the motivation. I had a hard time to continue paying the price for success – which is very high – in extreme sports. True, by then I had other goals regarding my profession, but it was only then I realized just how demanding cycling really was. As a top athlete, one must not simply stop from one day to the next. The body has to be weaned slowly. The body's function have to get used gradually to the normal level. I am very aware of that. Still, at the beginning, I lacked the motivation to get on the bike. A two-hour training trip was already tedious for me, so I often took a shortcut home. For long years, cycling had been the focal point of my life. And all of a sudden, there was this void in my cyclist's heart. My priorities had changed. Sports shifted from being the focal point to being a hobby, by now it means a relaxing change for me to be out in nature. New goals, set on the business world, have since ruled my life. Goals which I want to achieve with the same consistency as I did my three victories at the Race Across America.

I have realized my goal, my destiny!

Who kindled the first fire? Who developed the Bowden cable so important to shipping? And who invented the light bulb? The names differ or cannot be found out any more as in the first question. But one thing all three people have in common: They were driven by their unrestrained will, by the vision to come up with something that would make life easier. In the case of the light bulb, it was Thomas Alva Edison. In 1880 he submitted the basic patent for the first light bulb. The path there had been stony. It took Edison 10,000 tests until he held his first light-emitting something in his hands. Edison was driven from the inside, as are many successful people. Driven by the need and the power to transform his vision into reality. Thousands of tests failed, but he never stirred from his path.

My experience has shown me
to only ever disclose my plans and goals
when I am a hundred percent convinced about them.
Otherwise, they will not be able to withstand
the negative influences from outside.

My own path has been stony, too. Often, I came up against my limits. As in the years of my childhood, when my family was torn apart by strokes of fate, or when, in my mid-20s, I had to reconcile the quadruple burdens of family, profession, sports and school. My friends had fun in discos and clubs, as befitted their age. I hardly ever went out, thus I earned the epithet "house-mouse". I have never seen myself as an unsocial or stubborn person, it was just that in those times, my life had a different focus. I wanted to go to the United States and win the longest cyling race of the world as the second European to do so, at any costs. In hindsight I know I only managed to achieve this goal, because I was absolutely convinced of it. Of course there always were obstacles, be they financial, organizational or external influences ("You're not going to make it"), which were anything but motivating. Therefore stick to your own and personal goals and believe in them always. Don't be put off by setbacks or if you stumble again and again. Think of Thomas Edison, who saw the light-bulb shining before his inner eye and who constantly searched for new ways to make his vision a reality. You know the saying: It is not shameful to fall down, but it is not to get up again! You always have to find one argument more why it will pay to go on. Many people let themselves be distracted by problems that occur on the way to achieving their goal. The art lies in finding the right path towards those goals and to stick to it consistently.

It is better to plan less and make this actually happen!

To set goals, to achieve goals, these have become slogans used almost too often, without having any effect anymore. You can find them in almost every company motto. And the only ones who really work for the consistent achievement of the goals are the company's managers themselves ...! But for me, this sentence has an elemental meaning and contains the following key message: To set goals is of enormous importance. The only question is, how many! Set yourself fewer goals. Do not plan to lose weight today, quit smoking tomorrow, become a millionaire the day after and establish world peace next week. This, for certain, is not going to work. Formulate realistic goals that you can actually achieve. If you have a number of goals, set priorities. For example, if you want to lose weight: restock your refrigerator, change your eating habits – away with calory-rich in-between-snacks, change to a balanced fruit and vegetable diet. Go shopping with a clear plan and be aware. Buy running shoes or other sports equipment and exercise once or twice a week. Of course there will be times at the beginning of this period of change where you will want to bang your running shoes against the wall; this will be if there is no visible success within a short time, if the scales simply won't budge and thus you lose your motivation. Don't give in! Don't leave the path you have chosen! Often it is the small steps that will carry you forward. And sometimes they take you along a rough path. Nothing is handed to you on a plate, success doesn't come just by chance, often you have to work for it very hard! Once you have chosen a goal, answer the following questions to yourself:

- **What exactly do I want?**
- **When do I want it?**
- **How much do I want?**

We always find more reasons not to do things than we find to do them!

Each one of us has visions and goals today, other ones tomorrow, and new ones yet again the day after. What follows is that more and more goals and wishes accumulate, but none can be achieved, because you set yourself too many of them. One goal is pushed aside by the next one. This carries the danger that you expect too much of yourself. Therefore, plan less but translate it into reality the more consistently. A tried and easy measure is to write down your goals. All you need is a piece of paper and to start formulating your short-, mid- and long-term goals. What do I do next week, next year, and where will I be in ten years' time? A Wolfgang Fasching would note down the following with a smile on his lips: I am going to sell 168,000 books by 2010! You can elucidate on your visions, three to four pages. When I practiced this adapted "Hull technique" for the first time, I was sitting in front of an empty sheet for half an hour and was thinking about my goals. Then the dam broke loose, and I scribbled down four pages. After one or two weeks, I edited my wishes and summarized them on one and a half pages. Then you have to write down your wishes every day for the next six weeks! And by hand, do not type them into the computer! If you constantly write down your visions and goals, you identify with them much more. If you only think about your goals and don't internalize them, you will forget them all the sooner. This method is a kind of self-fulfilling prophecy. When you write down your dreams and visions every day, there is a high probability of their coming true one day!

The appeal of the goals

I have so far almost always reached my goals, because I was infected with them to the deepest fibre of my heart. And this is exactly what many people lack! When I want to achieve something, I have to be 100% convinced of it! Of course I had training sessions in snow and rain, but on the horizon there always was the image of myself realizing my project. The enthusiasm and joy of it nothing could take from me, neither temperatures below zero nor cold toes! In the course of my career, I had an incredible number of visions, but some of them never made it to a goal but instead gathered dust in a drawer due to lacking appeal. I crossed Australia by bike, as I did the USA eight times. Originally, I had wanted to cross all five continents by bike, but this never made it into a proper goal. What was missing simply was the appeal.

When people ask me today why I did not cross Asia or Africa, my reply is, "I don't know. It simply did not appeal to me!"

People can only be happy and content
when they deliberately plan on being so!

Short- mid- and long-term goals

As is generally known, there are three times of goals:

- **Short-term** – one to two weeks
- **Mid-term** – six months to two years
- **Long-term** – five to seven years

Short-term goals are meant for the next few days or weeks or even only for one special event. The goals should always be clear and specific: tomorrow I'm going to run 30 kilometres, the weekend I am going to recover in a spa, go hiking with my family. You need a lot of small, short-term successes to keep up the motivation for the bigger and more difficult goals. Even if success is very small, it strengthens our self-respect and heightens our self-confidence. This is familiar to us from soccer, when a soccer player says after a match, "The goal is giving us self-confidence for the next champions league match."

Mid-term goals stretch across a period of up to two years and should be written down. Personally, this book you're holding in your hand now has been a mid-term goal for me. An athlete builds up his annual planning based on the season's highlights, and holidays are mid-term highlights that need to be planned for each of us.

The long-term goals are those which regard complete planning of life or profession: whether you want to build a house, found a family or set up your own company. Such long-term goals you ought to write down by hand as described in the "Hull technique" above. Big plans can only be achieved via short- and mid-term goals. Use these to feed on motivation and check on your progress. My life has so far been shaped by a few big goals: by sports, my family and my professional life after my career as a cyclist. As of 1988, the Race Across America was my first long-term vision in the field of sports. Day after day, week after week, month after month I got myself inch by inch nearer to the goal by training and competitions. I increased the scope of my training and the number of competitions continuously. First I started in small races and there got my experiences of success and my motivation by winning. Those little highlights I saved in my subconscious. I could continually draw new power from these successes. A few years ago, a further vision started to manifest itself in my head: to share my experiences and knowledge with other people. From small slide shows I worked out seminars for well-known companies and organizations in the German speaking world. My long-term goal in this area? The foundation of a school of motivation ...

You have to demand what is impossible
to achieve what is possible

Often, it isn't enough to simply formulate your goals and write them down. "I am going to be a millionaire in two years' time" does not work. It is up to you to bring the short-, mid- and long-term goals up to scratch and to pursue them consistently. You have to determine the path, the speed and the strategy yourself. And keep out what is unrealistic! If you have a good business going as a retailer, don't think about confronting Microsoft with a plan for an unfriendly takeover in two years' time! I for my part always wanted to participate in the Race Across America and would not have been able to compete in the Tour de France. A Mr. Fasching is not a Mr. Lance Armstrong. My powers lie in the extreme endurance and not in classical cycle racing – two completely different disciplines – this I already realized in my early years!

Make your goals measurable and tangible. Your brain loves definite terms, so give it numbers! If you say you want to become rich, you must not contend yourself with this sentence alone. Think about the energy you are prepare to invest. Set a fixed amount of money you want to earn in the first month, in the second year, in the third year, in the first five years. Think carefully about what you are prepared to do to get this sum, and ask yourself whether with the energy and expenditure you invest you are able to realistically achieve this goal. Or if you want to lose weight. Set yourself a period of time within which you want to lose the desired kilos. Don't content yourself with mediocre goals like, "I'm down to 61 kilos already instead of the planned 60! That is quite enough!" Check your progress thoroughly and be insistent. Then the desired results will present themselves.

Leave the comfort zone!

In 2004 I made a dream of mine came true that I'd had for a long time: I passed the test as a helicopter pilot. During the three months training I studied a heap of books and spent approx. 40 hours in the helicopter with my teacher. After the training was completed, I continued to book flights with my flying instructor. I wanted to improve my flying skills and my stability up in the air. One situation of that time has stuck particularly: I was sitting in the helicopter, steering straight ahead. I felt like a retired Sunday driver with a hat on – I was flying carefully, not too fast, no sharp bends, did not approach any mountains because of the prevailing wind. As time went by, I wanted to expand my flying skills and got interested in new manoeuvres. I asked my instructor, "What happens when I move the joystick sharp to left or right?" He simply replied, "Well, try it!" And I moved the joystick carefully but still in a wider radius than before, first to the left, then to the right. The helicopter instantly responded with strong manoeuvres which really frightened me. All those tomes of books about theory could not impart to me what flying really is about: freedom! I realized I had left the comfort zone. Practice now does not make me leave the comfort zone any longer when I do such manoeuvres. In order to improve, no matter in which area, you have to be willing to take a calculated risk and leave the comfort zone.

Most people only want things they can do.
But they ought to be able to do what they want!

The comfort zone describes an area of safety which is seldom left. This area – like, for example, a job in an office one does for 20 years, or a relationship lasting 30 years – is not necessarily to be seen in a negative light. But each one of us wants to get on in life. You can only get on if you get out once in a while. A very good example for this from the field of endurance sports is the pulse ranges: there is the aerobic threshold which normally lies between 120 to 150 beats a minute. If an athlete always only trains between these values, (s)he will always remain medium. In order to be able to run faster, the athlete has to exceed these ranges. What is important here is not to exceed the range permanently but to always return to the lower range and pay attention to recovery periods. If you are constantly outside the comfort zone, the consequence in daily life is stress, overtaxing and, in the worst case, burn-out. In a sportsman's life it leads to over-training ...

An idea has to have the chance to become reality,
or it is only a vain bubble. Berthold Auerbach

Don't stop, continue your development. Attend educational training courses! When the end of my career got closer and closer – this started approx. 2 years ago – the first thoughts about a time after cycling started to swirl in my head. I already knew then that my goals and visions would lead me into the field of lecturing and seminars. For a few years now I have been attending educational training courses, did a training with the most acknowledged coach of rethoric in the German speaking world, attended courses at the College for Mental Training in Bregenz. I want to improve, too, and I have a positive and optimistic outlook to the future! I visualize my goals daily: I imagine how, in a few years' time, I will be the head of my School for Mental Training, how I give mental support to sports stars, how I support personalities!

Not at any expense!

How far are you prepared to tax yourself to reach a goal? How far are you prepared to put up with and accept the expenditure you face on your path to reach a goal? We must be aware that every realization of goals is tied to expenditure. When I started the College for Mental Training, a university course, in Bregenz in October 2006, I did not know what I was facing. The studies are structured into weekly modules. At the first information meeting we students were told what to expect. I brushed this off lightly and plain and simply underestimated it: Oh, it won't be as bad as all that! But the time and effort I had to give really was enormous during the months that followed. If I had known what I would be up against before starting the course, the price to pay might have been too high for me.

The biggest version is useless if you don't put it into action.

In the initial phase of each of my eight Races Across America there always was the same scenario reeling off in my head: After the first 200 or 300 kilometres I allowed myself to think about what lay ahead of me in the following seven or eight days. I asked myself the simple question, Yes or No. Do I want to do this race or not. I always answered that question with a Yes and never permitted a No. The consequences of a No would have involuntarily meant failure. I survived those initial phases of all my projects and pulled them all through with 100% commitment. From this time on I simply did not admit any negative thoughts any longer. Many competitors got off their bikes after 2,000 or 3,000 kilometres. Unthinkable for me, apart from rough external influences like falls, illness, etc. Once I made 3,000 km, I will make the other 3,000 km as well! You have to be brave enough to say No, even if a lot is demanded of you. Don't content yourself to wait until something works more or less smoothly. If your inner voice struggles against a plan, if it blocks you, then be brave and take the risk and say, "It's enough!" The price is, the stakes are too high!

The chronological guide to success:

- Identify your strengths
- Find your goals that you formulated yourself
- Your goals have to be realistic
- Work on them consistently and with ambition
- Ignore external influences, there will always be highs and lows.
- Think positive and check your goals
- Celebrate successes

FAITH AND MOTIVATION

How crazy has a man to be to master the last 200 kilometers of the world's longest cycling race with a broken rib? This was not a question I asked myself, I only heard it asked all the time. It happened during the 3rd Race Across America, in1998. I already had more than 4,600 kilometres in my legs, had only slept 8 hours during the previous 8 days and burned an average of 18,000 calories on each of those days. After a poor first third, I started to hunt the others down and had a cycling duel in the last third of the race with the Australian Garry Tatrai for the top position. In this advanced phase of the race, my body no longer was in a very fit condition. But after the victory of the year before and a third place, I wanted to make this double. In this Race Across America I learned one main thing besides my high pain level: Never lose faith in yourself – even if the situation seems hopeless. On the wet track I slipped at a track separator and fell on my shoulder so awkwardly that I broke my collarbone. The shock was clearly reflected in my face and the faces of my attendants, the first capitulation at an RAAM seemed impending. But so close to the finish? The last 200 km of the race can be compared to the blink of an eye within 24 hours. 200 km, that's nothing in the life of an extreme athlete. A hectic rush set in. I asked my physician, "Can I continue without problems? If I do continue, will there be a lasting damage?" My physician replied that if I could bear the pain, there was nothing to hinder me from finishing the race.

I agreed and got a knapsack bandage which we improvised with a sheet out of the camper. With the support of my crew I managed the last 200 km, with a little less speed, only one hand on the handle bar and the other bandaged up. Victory had moved beyond my reach. All that mattered to me now was to fight for my second place. I let triumph slip through my fingers, but I had the assurance that you can move mountains when you are highly motivated and when you believe in yourself! I still remember clearly my first thought after the accident. It was not, "Now it's all over. How could this happen?" It was, "How can I get to the finish as fast as possible despite of this?"

To the topic of motivation I could cite countless other examples. There is one I won't keep from you: In 2003, I started for the first time in the XXAlps, a 2,000 km non-stop race across the French Alps. It lead over 47 alpine passes with a total of 53,000 metres in altitude difference. My fiercest competitor was Andrea Clavedetscher from Switzerland. Right from the start, the Swiss set an incredibly fast pace, while I for my part remained relaxed and only concerned myself with my state, cycling my own speed.

He made a grave mistake: Clavedetscher bundled up all his power and concentration onto me. This means he adapted his sleeping hours to mine and continued through the first 3 nights without sleep! This mistake made itself felt in the finale. He wasn't doing his own race, his own rhythm; instead, he was always near me in his mind. On the last few kilometers, on the last but one pass, La Bonnete (with 2,802 metres the highest pass in Europe), he suffered a momentous slump and had to watch me – at this last but one pass, a few kilometers from the finish – snatch the trophy from right under his nose. He was broken, lost all motivation. Rien ne va plus, as the phrase is in roulette. Whoever loses faith in himself and his abilities thus reduces his own powers. Clavedetcher made the mistake to only concentrate on me and not on himself.

It is not the things themselves that worry us
but the conception of the things.

How often do we hear colleagues say that face a task that seems simply undoable, "I cannot manage, I cannot do this!" No matter whether it is to draw up a business plan or get through a job interview. Unshakeable faith in one's own powers is of enormous importance in every walk of our daily life. Belief is the basis on which to build motivation. Nobody can be motivated for a task (s)he does not believe in, of whose usefulness (s)he is not convinced. "If you want to build a ship, don't call men to gather wood, prepare tools, distribute and break down single tasks; teach those men to long for the vast, endless sea." This is an impressive description of motivation, written down by Antoine de Saint-Exupéry in "The Little Prince". But in order to be able to motivate yourself, first you need faith. Faith in yourself, in your goal, in the energy all around us.

So faith in a goal, in a thing, is the prerequisite for motivation. Motivation is a state of mind which always sustains the will – to turn a goal into reality. If I am not motivated, if I forego training today, I won't be successful tomorrow. How is this motivation roused? There are thousands of motivation coaches and special literature dealing with this topic. I am convinced that one can only achieve one's goals when one carries a tiny spark of motivation inside (internal motivator). Motivation has a lot to do with continually asking yourself, "Am I still motivated? Do I still want to be in this job? Does this company suit me or do I suit the company? There is nobody on earth who is able to convince me of a thing or to motivate me if I myself am not convinced of it! Motivation thus is closely linked with interest. When I was still an active athlete, I was often asked how I motivated myself when I cycled across America for more than a week without hardly any sleep. It is easy: there is a distinct goal and 100 % interest to reach this goal! On the endlessly long highways, passing through the most desolate areas of America, many of us would wonder, "How far is it till the next bend?" My inner question was, "How much have I covered already?" You all know the saying "a glass is half full or half empty" – how full or empty is the glass for you?

Once you know what you want (thus once you have a goal in your mind), once you have balanced the pros and cons and are convinced of your idea (thus believe in it), then you are ready to start making it happen (motivation). Often, goals are connected to wishes that are hard to fulfill. This can be, on the one hand, money, fame or honour, on the other hand, it might really be personal satisfaction and enthusiasm – for example, a hobby – which takes the fore. In the end, motivation is nothing but the sum of the reasons that influence your actions.

„When I know what I want, what I want to achieve together with my team, my employees, then I am motivated and ready to endure hardships!" And hardships I had a-plenty with all my projects. I distinguish two kinds of motivations: motivation coming from inside, and motivation based on external influences. The one far more important is the one caused by interest inside: you take steps because you want it, because you have decided to pursue this goal. You want to run a marathon and know that a lot of training is required for this. You will motivate yourself to get up one hour early each day so you can go for a run. You want to conclude an important business for your company but know that it is touch and go. You will work overtime, do some additional research and go to the meeting prepared to the brim.

If you are motivated by other people, external pressure, maybe by threats of punishment (external motivation), this does nothing for your performance and does not last very long. If what your friends and colleagues say refers to topics that are important to you, they give a positive impulse. "You have focused on this competition for weeks. It is looking great, your performance curve is going up. It is simply wonderful how you can motivate yourself. And soon your goal will be reached!" is an example for motivation coming from the outside.

Giving a good example …

Many people can only get motivated when the person they relate to closely has charisma and gives an example of how things ought to be done. Your employees will not show much engagement if you as their superior or manager don't also work hard. If the boss does not work overtime and is to be found on the golf course at six pm, why then should the employees be in the office implementing projects? The person to relate to has to give a good example: work overtime like your employees instead of spending the evening with friends. You cannot demand additional tasks from your employees, be conspicuous by absence yourself and on top of it send them holiday greetings.

You will not manage to motivate anybody by this method of work! This would be an instruction for the opposite, namely demotivating of employees. It is worse, however, if you yourself are not motivated and constantly moan and complain. The truth is: every company has the boss it deserves. And the same goes for the employees! Motivation problems can also be found in families: it will be difficult to keep your pubescent offspring from smoking if you point out the damages this addiction can inflict and do so with a cigarette between your own lips! Give a good example – an old phrase that, however, has not lost anything of its conclusiveness. To motivate others isn't grey theory but lived practice. "I cannot motivate myself." – Delete this statement from your vocabulary and your thoughts!

The starting kick

Motivation is all very well. But how do I put this into practice? With routine things in life, with seeming trifles, this normally happens automatically: once I start a task, I do not finish in between. It becomes more difficult with plans that mean a severe decisive point in life. How, for example, can I get rid of superfluous kilos? Many people who want to lose weight work themselves through books. They sit comfortably on the sofa and start to study various dietary theories. The right hand holds the book, the left hand continuously grabs the crisps bag. Do you think that is the right way? Approach the matter differently! Don't put the negative things to the foreground. Don't see in your mind's eye how you jog a few kilometers, panting, or how your fridge overflows with fruit and vegetables. This will also put you in a bad mood, because you are only allowed to eat things you don't even like! Be aware that the path towards the goal is not always fun. It is a lot of work to make kilos disappear. And therefore envision the end result: I can move more freely, I have more sex appeal, I can suddenly wear jeans I always had to pass by in the shops. Motivate yourself by the result and ban negative thoughts! Let's take running as an example: Once you set out in your running gear, only plan a 10 minute run. Ten minutes only? – you're going to ask. Yes, indeed, ten minutes only. You will see the time fly. So fast you won't want to stop after ten minutes. After two weeks, you set yourself a new goal: 20 minutes. After that you will smile on the ridiculous 10 minutes. Increase the distance and the time, and the result will be worth while!

Motivation, from the Latin ,to move',
means that kind of energy
everybody has at his disposal to achieve certain things.

Many obstacles accompany us on our way to our goal. If you want to lose weight, you will always face situations where you grow weak. Chocolate really is delicious! It is not forbidden to eat a piece now and then. But don't lose sight of your goal! And besides, apples, strawberries & Co. also have a sweet taste! There will always be doubts, setbacks. Never ask yourself, "How the heck am I going to manage?" If you are yourself convinced you won't make it, you won't make it. When I'm asked, "Mr. Fasching, how can you cope on only 8 hours of sleep a week?", I reply, "I can do it! I know that if I want to win the Race Across America, I have to reduce the hours of sleep to a minimum. And an hour of sleep per day is my minimum."

In the course of the years, this fact turned into a habit more and more. In my first endurance race it wasn't a matter of course to sleep for a few hours only. But I kept repeating to myself that it would be enough. And thus it was enough! Because when a person believes in this and is convinced that (s)he can get by on very little sleep, then (s)he will get by on very little sleep. But if you are convinced you need a lot of sleep, it will be so!

I don't give my weaker self a chance,
then I won't have to constantly fight it!

The weaker self

Who isn't familiar with this situation? You have planned something that is not quite so easy to achieve. For example, to lose a few kilos, an additional project, better performance with running or cycling. The goal is there, so is the faith in it, the motivation and the best intentions. And all of a sudden, there it is: the weaker self one needs to fight so often. It already speaks up in the morning ("Ah, I can stay in bed another five minutes, I can leave out breakfast"), at work, at the studies or in a relationship. The weaker self suddenly straightens itself up on your way to realize your goal. Very often in cases of stagnation, if there is no progress. Sometimes, the weaker self manifests itself in the so-called postponing technique, and one doesn't even start the realization of one's plan. "Next week I'm going to eat less." You have to fight and beat your weaker self if you don't want to slacken your good intentions. Often you have to take severe measures. You have to overcome resistance – not just once but over and over again over a long period of time. The prerequisite for this is basic discipline. If you want to go for a run and your neighbour asks you in for a drink, what are you going to do? The ideal case would be if you went for your run and looked in at the neighbour's later. Don't postpone your plan.

Just acknowledge your weaker self and even welcome its existence! This does not mean that you should become lazy and let your good intentions gather dust in a drawer. In those areas that mean a lot to you, you have to fight it without compromise. Show your weaker self your fist. But in other areas, you can let it do its work. If you celebrate with friends at home, for example; empty a bottle of wine or two and just enjoy yourself. Or if you stroll through the streets after work and feel puckish. Why ever not? Treat yourself with a clear conscience and don't bear a grudge.

Those constant worries ...

Man is a worrier! Statistics show: we spend 30 % on thoughts concerning the past; 52 % of our worries are superfluous, 10% unimportant, and only 8% of our thoughts are justified! This means, strictly speaking, that almost 90% of our worries that burden our lives are unnecessary. Very clear numbers that should have us alert. What do we think about? That our neighbour has a bigger garden than I? That my brother earns more money and can afford a bigger car? That a colleague who works harder gets preferred treatment? Don't hide behind excuses all the time and don't always be on the lookout for who is to blame for your worries. Everybody is responsible himself for what he does. Give up the envy complexes and investigate yourself. Find out how much you actually invest in your life.

KNOWING YOURSELF

Many people think I am a lone fighter. But whoever crosses America eight times, cycles through Australia, manages the French Alps and the Pyrenees nonstop in 2005, needs a team. During my projects, I figure as the company manager, the project leader. There is an engineer who keeps my racing bike in good shape and deals with any defects; there is a physician who keeps me fit from a medical point of view; there is a masseur who loosens my tight muscles; there are chauffeurs for the attendants' cars; there is a speaker who communicates my performance to the world. Their motivation is me pedaling like mad and realizing our common goal: get from the west coast to the east coast as fast as possible, reach the finishing line. Like my team motivates me by supportive words and their services, I try to support them within my means, to show an interest in what they do. I chat to my colleagues via radio. I know: we are all in the same boat!

To be an example to others, it is of great importance to be convinced oneself of the things you do. Have an optimistic view on things. But to be optimistic, first you have to know yourself. I cannot plan an expedition up Mount Everest and at the end realize I have a fear of heights! I have to concentrate on what are my core competences. In my case, this was extreme endurance. I am an extreme athlete and can play out my strengths at those crucial moments when competitions go beyond the normal measure in top sports. This applies now and applied in the past. When I trained with my long-term training partner Peter Luttenberger in Styria, I soon noticed that I needed additional training sessions. Often I would cycle for a few hours more. And during my time as amateur cyclist I also had the feeling that the road races were too short for me. So I exercised a bit more after the competitions or cycled home from the races. I have never been a specialist in mountains or sprints. I wasn't bad at it, I could have paid more attention to those qualities during training. But what would have happened? I would never have reached the level I reached in long distances. At the same time, intensive sprint training to heighten the power of speed would have had a bad influence on my endurance. My special strength, extreme endurance performance, surely would have suffered.

Recognize your strengths and be proud of them!

Isn't it a fact that throughout our lives, only the weaknesses are constantly pointed out? "See to it that you improve your English", although you have a B in mathematics, but nobody mentions that. Or, "Don't eat so much", although the person has already lost 5 kilos. Or, "Can't you speed this up?", although the employee is already doing five projects simultaneously and this feat gets no word of praise. How can you find a positive view of life when all you ever hear is what is not OK and what could be done better? It was said about Henry Ford that there were few things he knew anything about. One day he made himself available to the questions of the people present. There was a phone on the table, and the manufacturer of automobiles had an answer to every question. He said, "Even though I don't know anything, I do know whom to ask to learn it." Ford knew his business, strengthened his strengths, worked on his weaknesses, but not at the cost of his strengths.

Always look for new chances and possibilities in your life. Stagnation is a step backwards, movement, seen optimistically, is progress. Always balance your strengths and weaknesses, recognize them. Do the following: Imagine you step out of your body. Watch your way to do things, how you react in different situations. Was what I said really necessary? Have I offended other people with it? As soon as you have recognized your weaknesses, you have to accept them and must try to improve on them. But don't do it at the cost of your strengths!

So how do you recognize your strengths? This has a lot to do with the ability to observe. One such method has been described above: observe yourself from outside! People who can identify with long-term goals will hardly have problems to recognize their own strengths. What are the things I do with love and affection? What turns out well? What gives me pleasure? On the other hand: Are there tasks I don't like doing at all, I might even have to be forced to do? Things that don't turn out well, that don't give me pleasure? Of course there are nicer things in a cyclist's life than sitting on the bike with temperatures below zero. But I also know that if I don't do this, if I don't also tackle the tedious obstacles, there won't be any success the following season. Regarding training in below zero temperatures: I also have to adapt my body to extreme temperatures. An RAAM isn't only held in beautiful weather, differences in temperature of up to 50 degrees demand everything from the body.

If you are not satisfied with yourself,
the world will not bring you any satisfaction.

To recognize your strengths it is also important to find out how much time you spend on certain tasks. Do you have a job that makes a lot of demands on your time but does not fulfill you at all? Where you constantly think about your hobbies or alternatives? Then you will hardly have time for the good things in life. Furthermore, you have to find out which activities you do with a high quality. Granted, not everybody has the chance to make his hobby his job; as in my case. Still, ponder these questions carefully and answer them. Help yourself to filter and enlarge your strengths. Through all my projects I got to know a lot of people who think like me. Or during my lectures about cave climbers, people who sail around the world, adventurers and people who accomplished extraordinary things I recognized their similar frame of mind. They had a goal and pursued it with strict consistency. Such people think in similar patterns, while the majority of mankind only wants what they can do already, anyway. But I am convinced they all should be able to do what they want. The challenge with this, however, is unproportionally higher.

Learning processes

To get on in life, learning is important. This starts in early childhood, when the toddlers ask questions to acquire knowledge. "Daddy, why do wheels turn? Mummy, why is the sky blue?" Asking and learning goes beyond school. On and on and on you are confronted with the sentence: You don't learn for school, you learn for life. How true!

In my career, I have basically experienced mind-expanding learning processes on three levels:

- **Learning by experience**
- **Learning through pain**
- **Self-taught lessons**

A proverb says: One learns by experience. However, you only learn from this when you also assimilate the experiences. One moment is fading fast, more, new impressions come along. So it is important to analyze the experiences: why did the negotiations fail? Why has my lover left me? Why did I only make second place? Don't simply go on with the routine, do ponder on what happened. But the analyses should not only cover defeats but also victories or moments of success! Was the triumph really perfect, or could it go even better next time? Also take a neutral look at your successes. Like Pyrrhus at Epirus. 280 B.C. he beat the Romans and bemoaned his severe losses: another such victory, and I'm done!" A victory always is a victory, but it might be only a Pyrrhus victory.

Experience is one thing, pain another. What you experience for yourself, mentally or physically, will burn itself into your subconscious. Few children like going to the dentist. We all had our experiences: like hearing the sound of the dentist's drill, always tied to pain; or getting too close to the fire. Your children gain more if you don't constantly shower them with what they must not do; it is better to explain why electricity is dangerous. In my first Race Across America I had first-hand bloody experience of learning by pain. It happened in the Utah desert, on my way towards Las Vegas. Horrible heat was a constant companion, I suffered from the scorching rays of the sun. I kept pouring water over my head to keep my head as cool as possible. I was wet for five minutes, five minutes later dry as dust again. But what I was not aware of at the time – the permanent flow made the water accumulate in the pad of my cycling pants. Combined with the extreme heat, my skin was badly strained, and due to the friction I got sores.

After 500 km, still at the beginning of the race, I already had an ulcerated posterior – a scandal! Due to my inexperience I did not tell the team physician of my problems. Furthermore, I was thinking, " What are my teammates going to say when I already have such problems now? We can pack up and go home at once, that way Wolfgang is never going to make it." Motivation in the team would have plunged towards zero, so I thought. My condition, of course, did not improve. On the contrary, it got worse and worse. After approx. 1,200 kilometers I could no longer hide the difficulties, which became more and more obvious, from my crew: I kept skidding about on the bike, I couldn't sit in the saddle any more, cycled on standing up. Then came the moment that had to come.

The pain became unbearable, so I confessed it all to my physician. And he replied dryly, "Wolfgang, why don't you tell us earlier? We could have treated your posterior then without much of an effort." My learnings from this: Had I told my attendants about my ulcerated posterior straight away after 500 kilometres, a lot of pain would have been avoided. The way I handled it, more than 3,000 difficult kilometers waited for me till the finish.

Everyone of us experiences pain daily. Be it the pain caused by an employee's evil sense of humour, bordering on mobbing, or physical pain as experienced by workers at a blast furnace. But you cannot only learn from personal experience, you can also learn from other people's experience. Be careful in this, though: when you get advice from strangers or third parties, check their validity. Or do you think a new employee hears all the information and rules of behaviour in the company within his first days at the new job, things that took the others years to learn? When I prepared for my Mount Everest adventure, I read alpine literature extensively and thus acquired some climbing know-how. I read about the experiences of famous mountaineers and tried to identify with those people. Including all the pain one has to face when climbing such giants. After the fact I can tell you that reading all those books had been worth its weight in gold!

Take the time to expand your horizon. Get literature when you tackle great private or business topics. When I did my helicopter license, right from the start I wasn't content with the ordinary tomes. I devoured books about flying. Reading is education, and it can lead you to the top not only on your way up. Your superiors will be surprised when you can talk with them about more than just work-related processes, and you won't be seen as a crank or "nerd". Of course literature also serves to educate oneself in special subjects. Don't believe that knowledge is power. It is applied knowledge that is power!

Strengthen your self-confidence

What about your self-confidence? Do you do the things you want to? Like little children show us every day? Children have almost boundless self-confidence. Everything is possible in their world: they can be kings, astronauts, princes or fire fighters. But in the course of their development, society cuts off piece after piece of their self-confidence. "You cannot or must not do this! You are a boy! You are a girl! Not you! You don't have the talent for it! Be realistic!" Don't let your self-confidence be taken away. You have to win it back little by little, otherwise you lose performance. You have to do those things you do not believe you can do.

TEAMWORK

Why the heck does Fasching take 13 people to the Race Across America? The answer is clear: without a well-working team, a crew well adjusted to working together, I couldn't have achieved most of my successes. As an athlete, I am a lone fighter, but from the chauffeur to the engineer and masseur, every team member has his area where everything has to work to perfection. Just imagine Fasching going shopping during the Race Across America, because the refrigerator in the camper is empty! Without my companions, I would be without a chance in many situations. You can imagine the Fasching company like a bicycle chain: every link is of equal importance and there are no unimportant parts; only the positions of the links differ. And I see myself, the main character, as another link in this chain. I only have to think back to my last Race Across America in 2007. Till day four, everything was going smoothly. The speed was all right, and I was in second position behind Jure Robic. But then, on the fourth day, it really caught me with my pants down! It had rained for days on end, and I caught a persevering cold. The effect was fatal: there suddenly was a strain in my neck. First I thought this was a tensed muscle, but I could not keep my head up, had no strength in my upper spine, had problems with my neck muscles. I had not experienced anything like that in all my cycling career. I was sitting on the bike all tensed up and only tried to go on. The ordeal lasted for three whole days.

Ointments were applied to my neck, I got a neck support (Stifnek, which normally only is used on transportations into hospital). But I was not used to having an impeded view. With temperatures above 35 degrees, due to the pressure of the Stifnek, I chafed main parts of my neck area. I could neither look left nor right. Eating was massively hampered by the Stifnek, and each meal was torture. All I managed were tiny morsels. I only just managed to hold the drinking bottle with my lips and suck like that. Since I could not lift my head, I did not see any traffic lights nor intersections. I placed my fate into the hands of my attendants and had to trust them blindly! The only kind of orientation I still had were the white demarcations at the side of the roads and the line in the middle. The sightseeing was reduced to the grain size of the asphalt and the nuances in colour of the white demarcations and middle line. Due to the constant treatments I had to undergo and for which I had to get off the bike, the racing rhythm was broken. And on top of all this, the pursuers were on my tail. The situation was hopeless and frequently dangerous. It was only thanks to the devoted shouts and directions of my crew that I was able to continue and my hair-raising journey towards Atlantic

City and survive it without any further harm! During the race I realized that this problem would not improve under stress. Even though the situation was a nuisance, I never thought of giving up. Our common goal was Atlantic City. And we made it there! I am perfectly aware of it: I could be the world's best extreme cyclist. Without my team, I would never make it to the east coast!

My job of the next 12 hours is to drive the pace car and fix any flaws that might occur on the bike. As the sales manager for my area I am responsible for the sales of installation material. It is our common goal to get to the east coast of the USA as fast as possible. Our common financial goal is a sales increase of 50%.

A project like the Race Across America not only comprises the physical and mental training in the preparation phase, it also includes the organization. One year in advance I had already started to put together a team that would be able to face the challenges in America. As the cyclist, you go through the scenario a lot of times in your mind. Because a working team can make the race easier for you. On the other hand, a badly tuned team can cost a lot of time. Any team member is continuously busy from the moment of departure but at the latest from the start of the race. While on the journey, you cross three time zones. Your biorhythm goes haywire, because you get so little sleep. Add to this all the stress of the race. Eleven team members are constantly driving three cars, with a passenger helping with the navigation. This is the latest possible moment when you realize that a strict division of the tasks is impossible. Even if each team member started with a certain job assigned to him, it is important to see beyond one's own nose and also do tasks that lie outside the allocated job. It might be necessary for a masseur to grab a spanner, or for an engineer to massage a neck.

Although I started at the RAAM so often, my team never was the same. I always had on board, except for the first year, a healthy mix of old hands and rookies. The old hands know how the land lies. They have experience, can estimate situations correctly. First time team members bring pep and energy to their work. Compare this to a well-run management. In the background, there is the boss, he has long-term experience and works away in the back. The modern and dynamic appearance comes from the junior director. He doesn't yet have the necessary know-how, but he keeps the company going. On their own, none of them would be able to elicit the best. Together, however, they are an unbeatable team.

I am the boss of our projects. Before I start, I thoroughly select the crew members. I see to it that it is almost exclusively specialists in their fields who accompany me. Top priorities are a common language and a common goal: Do we all mean the same thing? Do we all pursue the same goals? Such questions might sound trivial, but they are necessary. Because each team member has his own character, a different perception. And therefore it is essential to check whether we all go into the same direction! The team must harmonize and be on the same wavelength. A team has to function down to the smallest unit. I am glad we have so far always managed to put together ideal teams. Be it job or family, where raising the children is the aim, be it building a house or planning future projects.

Not alone but together we are strong!

A team in a company is set up, because everybody has strengths and weaknesses. Be aware that other people might have their strengths were you have weaknesses. Thus teams are formed. Since not everybody in a company or family can do the same thing, tasks are divided. It is the core of a team that makes the decisions. Outsiders are drawn in to do certain jobs. In a team, every member is of the same importance. If one person drops out, the project can be at risk. This means there are no important and unimportant members in an organization. The CEO, the department head, the secretary, the cleaning staff: they all have to do their jobs within their means. Of course, some people take more centre stage than others, but nevertheless, every team member should feel important. Who likes to work in a dirty office, for example?

Meanwhile, I am giving numerous lectures at big companies. In such situations it is always nice to see when employees don't show off their achievements but talk about how great their company is doing. The bosses of such companies can really be proud of their employees. Identification with the company comes from deep inside and is honestly portrayed. With this kind of fire, company visions and goals can be ideally implemented. On the other hand, I always meet bosses who complain about their employees. These people I have to tell politely but straight that the employees can only ever be as good as their boss. The saying "The fish rots from the head down" hits the mark. Imagine your department head coming to work day after day in a bad mood and late. He hardly delegates, is either too bossy or treats the employees like bond slaves. Are there failures, he always blames the others. Are there successes, he prances about the room and says, "Look here, that's how to do it! It's to my credit!" Quite honestly, would you go through thick and thin with such a superior? Commit yourself to him 100%? Hardly ...

In all my projects, the goal was always clear: we give our best! We want to win, but we don't let ourselves fall under the pressure of having to win. It's the same in business. There have to be clearly stated goals and standards, and everybody has to know them! The director has to give a good example, show engagement and work goal-oriented. This is the only way to spread enthusiasm to the staff. Successes must not only be in the boss's charge. Everybody ought to share them. It was, after all, the whole team who worked on the project. Success has to be passed on to every single member of the team. Money is not always the right way to motivate. Personal praise and appreciation or a simple but honest "Thanks" strengthen people for further tasks. There is no difference here between sports, daily routine and the job. Any company can only be as good as the boss's example. And being the boss, I have to constantly try to motivate my employees by my own example.

Once, during the preparations for the Race Across America, I envisaged a certain physician who would have fitted in well with the team. In the course of the preparatory talks we defined his tasks. But after a lot of consideration, he doubted his abilities more and more. "I don't dare do this!" In hindsight, I was glad of his decision. He was brave enough to say No. If I imagine having a physician in my team who feels completely overburdened, how can I trust him 100%? As an employee, I also need to develop the ability to assess myself. Overburdening inevitably leads to a breakdown. Not being challenged enough, on the other hand, leads to demotivation. If I assess myself correctly, I know where my abilities and strengths lie, and thus I will enjoy my work much more in the long run.

Work alone, add up.
Work with others, multiply.
Chinese proverb

In the beginning was the vision.

I defined my goal, my objective.

There are more reasons not to do something than to do it.

Demand the impossible in order to achieve the possible.

Visions only make sense when translated into reality.

Focus upon yourself.

Live in the here and now.

Be a good example to follow.

The way to your goal is often bumpy and arduous.

The strength of successful (wo)men lies in their subconscious.

Everything takes place in your head.

You want it? You'll make it!

THE SUBCONSCIOUS

In May 2001, I was not to be found on the bike reeling off my training kilometers as usual, but I was located wearing sturdy shoes and warm clothes in the Himalayans. The location was the "ABC" up 6,400 metres, the Advanced Base Camp of the Mount Everest. In the emptiness of the mountain formation, up the world's highest mountains, the ice-cold wind blew about our ears. The atmosphere was anything but inviting. We waited and waited in that dismal tent-scape, 16 days all in all, for the perfect weather conditions to start the climb up the roof of the world. It didn't take long for frustration and cabin fever to spread. Many other expeditions had followed suit and were feverishly looking forward to their great challenge. Temporarily, the sun broke through the clouds, and one colleague attempted the climb. Due to another bout of bad weather he cancelled his plan and was back in the camp with us two days later. The seemingly endless days worsened our mood. In addition, at such a height, the body doesn't regenerate too well. I felt myself getting weaker by the day, felt my body losing strength and substance. Often, my climbing partners and I would sit together in the big tent, eating and killing time. We swapped stories of then and now, of tragedies and experiences in the mountains. "Remember when this guy was swept along by an avalanche in the French Alps?" "During the climb up Nanga Parbat, we suddenly saw this hand lying on the path." "This guy froze to death in a crevasse in South America." Just negative stories all of them, which further depressed us. I, the alpine greenhorn, observed the experienced mountaineers telling their stories, and I always left the convivial gathering early on such occasions. Why? I knew that such stories settle themselves in the subconscious, fuelling the fear of failure. Do you remember your childhood? When I was a child, a long time to go till I would be a teenager, I was always allowed to stay up late on Friday evenings and watch TV. Glued to the television screen, I watched the murders in "Tatort" ["Crime Scene"], horror films and the naturalistic re-enactments of murders and robberies in "Aktenzeichen XY Ungelöst" ["File Number XY – unsolved"].

I was sitting there all tensed up, hands close to my ears, ready to cover them when the music got too creepy. The adrenaline level reached boundless heights. After every such wonderful TV evenings, I went to bed on shaky legs. On the way to my room, I fearfully checked every corner, and once in bed, I pulled the blanket right up to my eyes, glanced at the window and made sure at least three times that the bedroom door was well and truly locked. Did you manage to sleep well after such films? And what did you dream of? Certainly it wasn't about Cockaigne with tons of sweets and an easy life, of sweet little bunnies and funny comic characters ... you were frightened!

The same happened at the ABC. By leaving early, I switched off the horror film prematurely, so to speak. During those 16 days of waiting in camp one cannot expose oneself to unnecessary negative thoughts. Those are around all the time, anyway. Just imagining my sleeping place in the tent: face up, hardly any room to turn, the roof of the tent was 20 cm above the tip of my nose. And then all that background noise, the icy wind constantly knocking at my tent. There sure was no lack of negative influences, falling asleep was next to impossible! And the worst of it was: the others disheartened themselves with their own stories! If I let myself be intimidated by endless tragedies during the long days of waiting, how careful will I be later, on the climb, when I am confronted with similar situations? If, for example, I have to cross a snow slab, and the thought occurs: who has fallen off here before me? The higher I climb, what will I be thinking about? Determination is crucial in many circumstances, not only in climbing. And it is a brainchild. People who have no self-confidence will have to put up with performance loss. We must not make our lives unnecessarily more difficult for ourselves. When I am sitting in the base camp of Mt. Everest, I busy myself with things as positive as possible, as far as this is feasible in such an extreme situation. On arrival, all participants in this expedition had been highly motivated. But the closer day X, the more dampened all expectations. Statements like, "It's great to have come so far already!" Or, "Reaching 8,200 metres, that would be something. Getting up to the peak would only be an extra", such things were heard with increasing frequency. They are thrown in casually but influence everyone. Of course everybody wants to get up to the summit, of course everybody is motivated to get there. But when you sit at 6,400 metres and reshape your goal to 8,200, you won't make it to the total 8,838 metres, or only just. The mark to be achieved is impressed on your subconscious. And you won't reach anything beyond that mark – goal achieved, goodbye!

My third Race Across America participation, in 1998, I not only remember well because of breaking my collarbone in that final phase. This RAAM also went down in history as one of the hottest races ever. It was on the third day, I was crossing Texas. The temperature soared up inexorably, reaching unbearable 55 degrees Celsius. It was one of the hottest summers the state had ever been through. We people from Central Europe suffered terribly under such heat. The head wind was blowing like a hair dryer at full force, there was no real chance to cool down. The rules state that my attendants must only see to me four times an hour for one minute each. Right, so I tried to keep myself cool with lots of water. But there was the danger that all the water I permanently poured over my head collected my cycling pants and chafed my bottom. This was a mistake I made during my first RAAM in 1996, when I was close to giving up after 1,200 km with a raw posterior. Our possibilities were exhausted with ice cube bandages round the joints of the arms, the forehead and the neck. I bethought myself of mental powers and imagined covering myself with a cooling mantle that would protect me from the scorching heat. Since I've always suffered from high temperatures, I concentrated on this fact prior to a race during my mental training. I mentally acted out the heat scenario over and over again (I can feel the warmth on my skin/it is pleasantly warm/cycling is much more fun when the sun is out) and thus influenced my subconscious in a positive way. This mental trick worked, within a very short time I was able to concentrate on cycling again, go at the usual high speed and even managed to extend my lead on my competitors. This was exactly the situation where I could feel the power of the subconscious and use it to my advantage in the competition.

The subconscious does not only play a vital role in my case as an extreme athlete. If I tell myself that today is heavy going, that I can't find my rhythm, I complicate my task. Negative wording influences your subconscious the same way as positive wording does. You are responsible for the way you think. Note: the subconscious can be controlled. In all my 8 RAAM starts I performed the same scenario prior to each break for sleep and rest: I kept talking to myself in a positive manner and mentally prepared for the rest period which normally lasted between 60 and 70 minutes. I visualized that I would stock up on lots of energy, that I had a relaxing rest period ahead of me after which I would get up on the bike again refreshed, alert and full of energy. This positive manipulation of the subconscious can be applied in all circumstances. If you wake up in the morning and tell yourself that it is going to be a wonderful day, chances are that the day will indeed be wonderful.

When I was preparing for the Himalaya expedition with the goal of climbing Mount Everest, during my mental training I kept visualizing the image of the successful conquering of the peak. Up to five times a day I listened to my especially produced mental CD, especially during the period of waiting at base camp: I felt the wind which was blowing up on the peak in 8,848 metres and which penetrated my clothes, I saw myself standing on the highest peak on earth, I smelled the snow and the ice. Afterwards, I visualized myself coming down again as slowly and carefully and arriving safe and sound down below. What was important in this was not to allow any unrealistic images. The positive manipulation must not collide with reality. I did not suggest to my subconscious an image of myself eating ice-cream and wearing bathing trunks up on the roof of the world!

The only thing that counts is what you do,
not what you recommend others to do.

With the help of mental training, you can deliberately control your subconscious, feed it with positive thoughts. But beware, progress is slow in being felt! Don't expect the visualization and suggestion exercises to take effect at once. You will often have the impression that the training is good for nothing. Unfortunately, many people discontinue the training then, saying, "There's no use in this." But I say: Believe in the power of the subconscious. It is only when you believe and consistently work on it that you will reap the success due to you.

The power of the subconscious

The subconscious very likely is the most efficient instrument we have in our body. It is comparable to a computer's harddisk with unlimited memory space. Data are never deleted, regardless whether they are positive or negative. No matter which thoughts, opinions or impressions imprint themselves into your subconscious, they will come true and take shape! You can communicate anything you like to your subconscious. But it will only implement those things you actually plan to do! If you plan a 50 km cycling trip but after 20 km decide that 40 will be quite enough, you will have a hard time meeting your original goal. This is because your subconscious will say after 40 km: Stop, that's enough, goal met! We spend so many thoughts on the conscious mind and so few on the subconscious. We don't know how simply the latter works. It is only waiting to be fed, it is as with a computer: the subconscious is the software and determines what we do and how we function. Our subconscious registers what we see, hear, feel, perceive and experience. It not only reacts to things we perceive consciously but also to events or things we often aren't even aware of.

Health is like salt.
You only notice it once it's gone.

The subconscious controls all important processes in life and is responsible for the correct functioning of the complete organism. Unlike the conscious mind, it works day and night and is always accessible. Both types have one thing in common: they save all traumata, be they processed or not. Unlike the conscious mind, the subconscious does not depend on facts and logical coherence. It is the subconscious which brings you the nightmares after a nervous, bad day, or after a horror film. Fear of the unknown, the things to come, is transported and forwarded to the physical level: the outcome is shivering, breaking out in sweat, or clenching. It works the same way in a positive direction: as the physician and philosopher Paracelsus (1493 – 1541) already said, who recognized the enormous powers of the subconscious, "The physician can bandage the wound, but healing must come from the patient himself! The one who matters is the physician within." One area of the control of all processes in life that is exercised by the subconscious is healing. We all carry the "physician within". But his power has to be recognized! Illnesses are a cry for help by the organism, and we always consult the doctors when it is already too late, when the illness has already broken out. Each one of us who has his body under control has the ability to recognize early on little aches and pains that announce themselves. You don't get a fever overnight. The same goes for fever blisters. Such illnesses are short-term immunity deficiencies, the subconscious can activate powers of self- healing in such instances. As was the case in my 3rd Race Across America, in 1998. Right from the start, things were going "crappy"; that's how I felt then. It was horribly hot, and on the second day, there were signs of sunstroke. And in addition, joining my stomach pains came a fever! For a person having to spend the whole day on a bicycle, this is hell, of course. My attending physician told me succinctly on the morning of the second day, "Wolfgang, if the fever isn't gone by afternoon, you'll have to have a long break, or in the worst case you'll have to drop out of the race!" I told myself he couldn't possibly do such a thing. I was there to deliver a good race and not to give up on the second day. I kept talking to myself and persuaded myself that I was well, that there was no fever, that I had a lot of pressure on the pedal. The autosuggestions paid off. It happened: my subconscious saw to my being without fever in the afternoon. The power of your subconscious will also bring health to you! Powers will arise you would never have dreamed of!

The true power of successful people lies in their subconscious.

The true influence of the subconscious I got to feel during my Mt. Everest expedition. As a preparation of this project, I acclimatized on the Nyanchen Thanglha, a 7,117 m colossus in the Trans-Himalayans. It was a sort of test run, a personal qualification for the Everest. But on reaching Lhasa, I got a terrible toothache. The pain worsened with every day. I thought I had to go home again straight away. With such unbearable pain I could forget the project Mount Everest on the spot. Conditions weren't ideal, and I decided to go to a hospital. I found one, but it looked like a European hospital of 100 years back: spartan furniture, no x-ray machines. I was actually afraid and didn't have the slightest idea what the physician said to me.

Afterwards I returned to the hotel, dialed Austria and asked for a connection with my own dentist. Shortly before leaving for Asia, I had had a checkup, so the dentist opined it couldn't be anything bad, there could be nothing to it. "The pain is caused because of the altitude," he calmed me. I actually relaxed, and the joy of the adventure returned. I regained trust in my health, and the negative thoughts and the pains themselves vanished a few days later. With a few attendants, I left for the Nyanchen Thanglha's base camp a few days later and passed the qualification on the 7.000 m summit. Afterwards it was back to Lhasa for three days to wash our clothes, communicate with home and make the last provisions for the Everest expedition. In a jeep we drove to the first base camp on the northern side of the massif. From there, after a few days in the base camp at 5,300 metres, we set out to the two days distant "ABC" base camp at 6,400 metres. My tooth problems had vanished into thin air. On the one hand, this was due to my trust in my physician, on the other hand, I had found my goal again which had temporarily slipped from my sight and which I achieved two days later: I was standing on top of the world!

The subconscious, the powerful companion!

Already at an early age, our subconscious is getting occupied by suggestions. Most of the time they are of a negative kind: don't touch the stovetop or you'll burn your fingers! Put on a cap so you don't catch cold! Don't climb the tree or you will fall down! Don't step onto the street or something bad will happen! Why don't you try the following sentences for a change: Put on a cap so you will be warm! Don't climb too high in the tree so you can come down again easily! Mind the cars when you cross the street! Already at an early age, we are instilled with too much fear and too little self-confidence. The likelihood is high that what you formulate will happen. So try to delete negative trains of thought.

In most cases, you won't be successful, because due to external influences it is not always possible to ban all negative thoughts. But try to assign a positive wording to such negative thoughts. I was already fascinated by flying when I was only a little boy. I eagerly followed every plane that flew over my Styrian home with my eyes. Even then I knew that one day I would be sitting in a cockpit myself and handle a joystick. It took almost half a lifetime until I could realize my vision of flying. In 2004 I finally was the proud owner of a flying license. Of course I had doubts as a small boy: will I really be able to manage that? So don't allow negative wording to settle in your subconscious. When you go through life optimistically and openly, when you stick to your goals and visions, your subconscious is going to enhance your positive outlook on life!

Imagine yourself out on a golfcourse, playing after a fashion. The situation arises where you have to hit the ball across an acquatic obstacle. You're not doing well, one crisis follows the other. Now if you encourage yourself by saying, "I will not hit the water! The ball will not fall into the water" – your subconscious does not recognize the word "not". This abstract word cannot be converted into an image. Terms like "ball" and "water" can be converted, though, and they can be perceived by the senses. So prior to hitting the ball, try the following statement: "I am going to do a precise hit far across the water. The ball is going to land close to the green, and I am going to put successfully." The subconscious knows the words "ball", "hit", "green" and "flag". You will hit beautifully!

The "board example" has become a real classic by now. I always explain it in my lectures. Imagine a board lying in front of you, approx. 30 cm wide and 10 metres long. You will have no difficulties walking across it. Now put the board across a stream two metres up. Do you have problems crossing it now? And what happens if the board connects two slopes over a chasm, 20 metres up? Do you dare cross the same board that was lying on the ground not long ago? A game of golf and crossing a chasm are easily conferrable to other areas. If you equate a diet with "not eating", with hunger and an empty refrigerator, with exercising which you don't like, with an empty stomach, and with time you don't have, you will struggle to lose weight. But if you equate a diet with vitality, sex appeal, health, success and more pep, your chances of success increase dramatically. Describe your eating habits in as much detail as possible and establish an emotionally positive connection. When you envision your goals, phrase them emotionally and pictorially. And always do this. Dealing with the subconscious is an everlasting exercise! Day after day it is your task to amplify the positive power over the subconsious.

Strengthen your subconscious

The best times to influence your subconscious with positive wordings and thoughts are shortly before going to bed and shortly after waking up. These are the times when your subconscious is most receptive. In such moments where the past day is history and the new one hasn't started yet, you can influence your subconscious positively with affirmations (invigorating and strengthening words). Think about nice feelings you have had or about beautiful moments of the day. Think about the goals you have achieved or are going to achieve. And take up the feeling to be able to re-live positive experiences. Visualize these conceptions, imagine the pictures going with them, reel them off in your own cinema. Accompany this "internal film" with your favourite piece of music and try to smell your favourite fragrance. While you are asleep, your subconscious is continually busy with the programmed topics. The result will prove you right: You will wake up feeling fresher, more optimistic, more cheerful. A successful day starts with those thoughts you went to bed with the night before! So make sure to go to bed with positive thoughts.

Shortly after waking up, when I was still in a relaxed state and the subconscious still is receptive, I always thought about health, power, harmony, happiness, contentment. Simply my key words. Use your own personal words with their individual emphasis. One person concentrates on being slim, the other on being healthy. Never forget: the subconscious is your powerful companion! Change the content of your thoughts in the morning, at night, during the day, and thus your life will change also. Save pretty thoughts together with everything that makes you happy. Make use of the creative power of the subconscious that lives within you, and the strength will never run dry!

Discover the joy of constant training

Your motto should be: practice, practice, practice! Because only then you will improve. You cannot prevent it. At least you will improve to a certain degree. If, for example, I have absolutely no ear for music but still practice all the time, I won't become another Mozart, but I will improve. The joy in practicing, in the training, is vital here. I found out about this with running especially: at the start of the running season, it isn't much fun. That's why I don't start with a one-hour unit but walk and run in short intervals for a while. Once I make progress, find my rhythm more and more easily, it will automatically be more enjoyable. The correct dose is what matters!

The only proof of your abilities are visible achievements.

Visualize your thoughts!

Each one of us is able to control our subconscious in a negative or positive way. It works with images. Think about commercials. Adverts cannot be measures 100%, but the images they generate, symbolising, for example, freedom, success or individuality, are reflected in our subconscious. The commercials' mechanism of action still hasn't been found and is not tangible. Henry Ford coined the prominent phrase, "I know half of my advertising budget is a waste of money. I just don't know which half!"

Visualize your thoughts in your mind's eye! It sound complicated, but it isn't. Believe in your innate positive ideas and thoughts. They really do exist, and one day, if you stick to them unwaveringly, they will take shape. Form a clear and straight picture of what you want to achieve. This technique of visualization leads to the "internal film" again. You see yourself in a state where your reality has become true: you're sitting in front of the open fire in your new house, or you receive an offer for a well-paid job. You stroll around Venice with the love of your life, or you see yourself sitting at a job interview. To be successful means to live successfully. All states and conditions, like peace, harmony, health, love or happiness, are of mental origin and originate inside man's deep self. He who does not egoistically pursue his way but incorporates his fellow beings is a happy and content person. If you want to become a physician, for example, you must not content yourself with passing the last university exam. Your career only really starts afterwards!

If there are no visions in life to long for, to realize, then there is no reason to apply oneself.

Why is one person happy and another one not? Why does one person accomplish ingenious things and the other person does not? Why does one person survive an incurable illness while another one perishes from it? Why does that person live in a great and harmonious relationship while I languish from one affair to the next? The answer to all those questions won't come as a surprise: every man is the architect of his own fortune! But each of us has to give his share and has to think positive! Remember that your thoughts are saved in your subconscious and shape your life. Somebody who has no goals and constantly complains about the happiness of others will continue to stagnate, and nothing in his situation will change. Memorize your own keywords – like, for example, success, faith, happiness, health and contentment – again and again. In the course of my lectures I always get to know remarkable businessmen who always repeat the word "success" to themselves, and their success proves them right.

Rituals

Everyone in top sports agrees on the power and importance of the subconscious. By way of trained actions, top athletes can download the programs they saved in training for competitions. Take a slalom skier, who immediately prior to starting goes through the track in his mind's eye; with eyes closed, he uses his hands to simulate the route through the poles. Or a ski jumper, who nervously fidgets with his goggles before the jump, checks the binding for the umpteenth time and quickly crosses himself. By these actions which are seen as nervous fidgeting, the athletes are building up the necessary concentration and their area of tension. Rituals can also be found in the business world. Take a sales assistant who quickly smiles at herself in a mirror before she asks the customer to the cashier. Or a manager who always clenches his fist before he goes in to a meeting. The goal is the same in all these situations: keeping up the concentration, focusing on the essentials. Maybe you yourself have your individual rituals. Maybe you step out for a bit of fresh air to fill up your energy before you to into meetings?

Rituals are important in life to download stored suggestions. Key phrase: doing things automatically: it is about storing sequences of movements in the subconscious to be able to call on them time and time again. Even in daily life, a vast number of activities happen automatically. Just think back to your first driving lesson, to the play between clutch and gears. I am sure I'm not the only one who stalled the car repeatedly in those first driving lessons and who found this stressful. Today, I no longer think about that. The car seems to drive itself.

Rituals are often employed by the advertising industry. Here, the main aim is to spread suggestions. If you watch a commercial for a special product on TV, if you can place it visually and acoustically, if you know the slogan and also can connect it with positive experiences, all it takes for you is to see and hear the slogan "I'm loving it" (ritual), to in the end see the big, curved McDonald's M in your mind's eye (suggestion).

Rituals are also helpful in dividing different tasks. Take job and spare time. When you get home and put your briefcase into the cupboard, you thus leave your job behind the moment the door is closed. Or when you switch off your computer or close the office door when the working day is done. The activities themselves are not sufficient, what matters is that you become aware of such situations and associate them with an effect following from them: when I switch off the computer, that's it!

APPRECIATING YOUR OWN SELF

In 1999, I set a new world record: The trip "across Australia" I managed in 7 days and 17 hours. A few years later, in October 2001, I returned to Australia. This time, it was for a race in the northeast of the continent said to be the world's longest and toughest mountain bike race: the Crocodile Trophy. This race is characterized by a mixture of comfortable family atmosphere paired with ruthless bike-to-bike duels. Up to the last but third stage I was in promising second place in the overall ranking. Everything went according to plan. As in the week before, we camped out in the middle of nowhere, chose a nice spot on a meadow with as few snakes as possible, and put up our tent. Next to it, we made the fireplace. The bicyle was lying in the meadow as usual, right next to the tent. Basically no problem, but on that evening, a teenager tried his hand at being a lorry driver. No problem for me, but for my mountain bike. The teenager overlooked it and passed right across with this vehicle weighing tons. The bike was bust, it was useless for the last three days. I did not have a spare bike, so I had to accept the offer of the organizer, who supplied me with another bike. The problem with this was that it was much too small, had no suspension fork, and I did not feel comfortable on it. I felt it next day, when another stage through the North Australian desert was due, over stony ground and marshland.

My competitors started with incredible speed, I fell back without a chance right from the beginning. The overall ranking was gone, as was the joy of mountain biking. With hindsight, I should have looked the gift horse in the mouth, should not have accepted the organizer's bike. The point after my cycle crash in the Crocodile Trophy was not that I could not accept a failure. The point was mainly to recognize myself. A point was reached where I should have said No. This definite No would not have meant that I was unwilling but that I was unable!

A person who has found himself
can never again lose anything on earth.

Be honest with yourself! As a smoker who lies to himself by claiming he only smokes a packet a day, and in reality it's two. Or if you exercise, it makes a difference whether you enter 13.5 or 14 km per day into your training diary. The difference amounts to more than 150 kilometres a year, after all! Honesty with oneself is an important issue in order to rule one's body and mind and allocate oneself the right value in the various areas of life. It happens again and again that one wants to cover a little accident or mistake with a white lie. You tell a story, tell it again, and again, and again the following day, and you start believing it yourself. Thus one creates one's own truth!

If it isn't lies or white lies, it is excuses that keep us from seeing the truth as it is. You have to learn to recognize excuses as such and gradually stop them. Because hand in hand with excuses come doubts, and if those two combine, they divert us from our goal. Our endeavours can therefore only be to identify the truth. There is no room for lies in the life full of goals and visions you plan for yourself!

Live your dream and say goodbye to your excuses!

If you are not yet honest with yourself, a first step in the right direction would be to decide to think about it with every little dishonesty and formulate correct, honest replies. If you want to lose weight, consciously think of all the food you eat in the course of a day. And abstain from that piece of cake to your afternoon coffee – "That one piece can't be the reason why I don't lose any weight!" If you study for an important exam and fail in the end, admit to yourself that you left out a lot of topics ("Did he have to ask that? Oh, I won't be asked that, and I know it all, anyway!"). Or if you simply did not invest enough time ("student's job, girlfriend, spare time, exam stress ... who can reconcile all that?"). Also, if you want to quit smoking, be honest with yourself and think about how many cigarettes you actually smoked: was it five, seven, ten, or twenty? In the end, you harm none more than yourself and especially your health!

Talk to yourself!

The balancing act between honesty and dishonesty towards yourself is always a try to get something positive out of failures. There is the permanent danger of lying to oneself. On the other hand it is the same with successes. Only if you turn visions into reality for yourself, will you be successful. There is one thing, however, you must never forget: do blow your own trumpet! How often do I call myself an "idiot" who can't get anything right? "Why can't I do this?" "I'm doing the same stupid thing again!" „I'm too stupid for that!" Why don't you try the opposite for a change? Go ahead and praise yourself: "I did this well!" „I'm proud of myself!" or „This was good!" Everybody talks to oneself. Sometimes in public, which is very seldom accepted by our fellow-beings; but most of the time without realizing it. But talking to oneself is essential for us and a further possibility to feed our subconscious with positive "fodder".

„We like to give advice to others, why not to ourselves?"

In an athlete's life, mental training is of great importance. Basically, this is a kind of talking to oneself or suggestions. Nobody can do without talking to oneself. The more importance should be given to do so on a cultivated basis that can also be used for one's personal advantage. At the beginning of this book, I wrote about dreams and the achievement of the goals resulting from them. As a first step, you clearly define a vision. Then follows the announcement of your goal ("Want to hear the latest news, I'm going to be self-employed!" or, "Mum, I want to do the Race Across America!"). But such announcements are not always met with approval by the other side. If you mention a goal which seems unrealistic to other people but has taken root in yourself, we find very little favour. In extreme cases, you will ponder the arguments and finally put the goal back in the drawer. So before you talk about your goals with others, confront yourself with them first; weigh the pros and cons, discuss them with your inner self.

When I talk to myself, this does not necessarily have to happen in public. After my lectures, where I face an audience from a stage, I don't go and say, "Wolfgang, you did this marvelously!" That could soon leave a bad impression. I prefer deliberate talks to myself and self-praise when I'm alone, when I'm on my way home.

In all my years as an extreme athlete, talking to myself meant a lot to me. Imagine you cycle 5,000 km across America and nobody – except for short small talk with the attendant crew – talks to you. You would go mad. During a Race Across America I did not continuously talk to myself all the time I was alone. If I did talk, I encouraged myself, praised myself. The rest of the time, I did my mental training, memorized the license numbers of the passing trucks or added the miles to the next timing checkpoint.

I have already mentioned that you should delete certain words from your vocabulary. Now try the following: Get up in the morning and try not to use certain words any longer. For a day, only use "be allowed to" and not "have to". "I am allowed to go to work today" instead of "I have to go to work today."

CHANGE AS CHANCE

If the talk turns to visions, many people invariably think about the great visionaries of the past. Whether it be a Napoleon, who went into battle for France to make it a world power, or a Caesar, who would stop at nothing to establish the Roman Empire as a world power. There is a visionary in each of us, maybe only a small and modest one. Everybody has visions and goals that shape our lives and thus cause changes. I am no exception. I did an apprenticeship as a painter and as a retailer, spent four years in the army and managed a grocery. As an athlete, I was also constantly on the lookout for new challenges. I couldn't have imagined, as my competitor Rob Kish (USA, three-fold RAAM winner) did, to participate in the Race Across America 20 times. Eight times was enough for me! I concentrated on a number of races, like the XXAlps (2,130 km through four alpine countries: Austria, Switzerland, Italy, France; with 53,063 metres altitude difference – this meant a distance six time the one from sea level up Mount Everest!), the Crocodile Trophy in Australia (the world's longest and toughest MTB race), the Le Tour Direct (a non-stop race across France in the tracks of the Tour de France), the Race Across the Alps or, in 2004 and 2005, the Raid Extreme Provence, a mountainous one-day race in Provence, which was listed as the first official ultra-European championship. Even during my career as an athlete I tried to put out my feelers towards new possibilities, new areas. It was after my fourth start at the Race Across America, in 2001. I was looking for a new challenge and found the answer in my dreams. Mountains had been haunting me for a long time, though I had hardly had any experience in alpinism up to that time; apart from a trekking tour in Nepal, a few hikes in the Alps and a failed Aconcagua expedition in January 2000. Nothing much to go on, but the fascination of Mount Everest was strong enough to make climbing the world's highest mountain my new mid-term goal. This change wasn't an easy one, because up to then, I had only known mountains from a saddle perspective. I bought books and special literature, read reports by experienced mountaineers. At the same time, I set out for my first easy hiking tours and increasingly got better. Of course I had the physical prerequisites, but time was short, I only had six months to go from "hiking tourist" to serious mountaineer. I accepted this challenge, because it was big enough. Regardless of possible risks I learned the techniques to move about in ice and snow. Finally, climbing up Mount Everest succeeded on May 23, 2001, at one o'clock pm, and in doing so, I made a dream of mine come true. I was standing on top of the world and at the same time at a new beginning. What comes next? In the years to come I returned to cycling ...

During the last months and years of my cycling career I often asked myself: What are my long-term goals? Where will I be in 10 or 15 years' time? My short-term goal after the end of my career was to take time off for a year or two to relax. To compensate the hardships I had had to go through as an athlete. But I had to dismiss this plan because of my long-term goals.

I have started to establish a second foothold which by now has become my main job: to pass on to other people the things I have experienced and learned in sports and in my adventures.

Change, and the world will change around you!

Changes shape our whole life and are essential. Especially if you are dissatisfied with yourself and your situation in your job or private life. Change makes possible the development of each of us. Changes mean reforms you should evaluate without prejudice. To leave well-trodden paths means to find out other, better possibilities to do things. But what reforms mean most of all, is to throw off habits, to change! How hard is it for notorious nail-biters to let go of their vice? A folk saying goes, "There's nothing better in store!" We all know what it's like to be in a relationship going through more downs than ups, where quarrel is a daily routine. Most of us just give in, content themselves with the situation in the end, accept everything. But I claim: There is always something better in store! If you are unhappy, complaining all the time, you have to have the courage to modify your life. But please: only if you are unhappy! If you are happy and are satisfied with your job and your family life, leave it at that!

You are what you think!

Lean back and consider your life. Consider your daily life, your relationships, your professional demands. Maybe you don't enjoy your job any more, because you are mobbed by colleagues, because you have a boss who doesn't value your performance, or simply because you don't earn enough money. And how is your relationship? Going well except for minor squabbles that happen everywhere? And do you regularly meet your friends? If everything in your life is running smoothly, you can now stop reading and close the book. If it isn't like that, find the reasons for it. Have an open talk with your partner about the things that are going wrong! Ask for an appointment with your boss and mention all the things clearly that you want to change. If you don't ask for an appointment today, you won't ask tomorrow, either, and the day after tomorrow even less. You will resign yourself to your situation and think that "basically", it isn't going so badly, after all. Many people content themselves with their situation after all. Maybe it's due to the fear of losing one's job or of being left on one's own. But you have to be aware of one thing: If you don't communicate your requests, you will remain frustrated and thus also a burden for your fellow-beings! And another thing you must not forget: each positive change makes you richer in experiences and thus less afraid of new changes. A kind of positive vicious circle!

To me, top athletes and opinion leaders in business have a lot in common: both groups are subject to constant changes and accept them more easily. Successful sportsmen and managers can draw back on a great potential of experiences. Without consistency and continuity on the one hand and the will to change on the other hand they would never have reached their envisaged goal. Whether it is an athlete who sets a new swimming record or a company director who manages a successful business, they all accomplished things that are very far away for most people. I deliberately don't claim they are "beyond reach", otherwise, none of us would be able to reach such goals. All we have to do is see changes as something positive and as new chances.

Changes don't always have to take place on a grand scale. If you want to get divorced or give notice, please don't use this book as an excuse! It is not always necessary to immediately get divorced, change jobs or emigrate. Sometimes, a clarifying talk with the partner or department head will do. Sometimes, it is even enough if a soccer player asks for the chance to show his abilities in midfield instead of defense. If you really should lose your job, this is a change and at the same time a great chance. It is now up to you whether you evaluate this new situation as threatening or friendly.

You have to know where you want to go,
or you will end up somewhere else.

I already wrote about comfort zones in the chapter „Visions and goals". This is about that area where you feel comfortable, where no unexpected problems flood in on you. It is your personal castle where change hardly happens. In your comfort zone, if, for example, you experience the same routines day in day out – breakfast, work, coming home, dinner, TV, bedtime – you cannot develop. Imagine the whole world was a comfort zone: there would be no progress, no inventions, no visions, no goals. Everything would come to a stop, the economy would stagnate – and stagnation means a step back. Far too many people live in their own personal comfort zones and follow the crowd. They have set their goal not to be conspicuous. If man were meant to live in packs, this would be good. Once again, my motto applies: Most people only want what they can do. But they ought to be able to do what they want.

If you want to develop or change well-established habits, you have to leave that castle of your comfort zone. You have to enter an area where you might not feel so well and comfortable any more, but here is where development and change happen. How difficult changes can be, we all experience in our daily life. If I have done a thing one way umpteen times, it is very difficult to change this behaviour. I still vividly remember an example from my youth. We did not actually live on rice pudding, but we regularly had it on the menu. My mother was a specialist where rice pudding was concerned. She made delicious rice pudding and always topped it off with enough sugar. When I participated in my first races, of course I also changed my nutrition. Spaghetti and other noodle dishes displaced the sweet dishes. At that time, I often visited my mother, and she served – as usual – her delicious rice pudding. I asked her not to add the sugar topping. But she only said, „But it doesn't taste good like that, it's disgusting." We often had a battle of words, and they often resulted in her turning her back to me and quickly adding a spoonful of sugar to the rice pudding without my noticing it – or so she thought. She simply could not break her habit of serving rice pudding without sugar. Her comment was, "Rice pudding without sugar cannot taste good. You've always eaten it that way, after all!"

Take the risk

After my lectures in companies, sport clubs or institutions I often hear, „Wolfgang, you must be crazy. All those things you have done!" But where do you draw the line between what is colloquially declared crazy and what is drawn by a human hand? If I were to draw that line, it would certainly differ from common opinion. My projects were and are well planned and calculated; no sign of madness. I know I've always moved in border areas of my mental and physical performance, but I know my mind and body very well and know where my limits lie. I go even further and claim that I feel comfortable at my performance limits, because I can recognize and avoid the crucial step across that limit. Only people who constantly feel their way towards their own limits also get to know that area.

My risk awareness has particularly been sharpened by the Mount Everest project and the preparations in South America in connection with it. In climbing especially, you are impressively shown how many opportunities arise from even the lightest changes. By small increase of risk or small shiftings of position, you effortlessly are presented with further steps or grips. What seemed impossible a few moments ago is suddenly done. We are also confronted with such situations in our daily life. All you have to do is recognize the stagnation and face it with corresponding change strategies. In sports, the slogan is: attack or defense? If a 10,000 m runner who does not stand the best of chances in a sprint launches an attack 3 kilometres away from the finish, of course there is a danger that he cannot keep up his speed and will be caught up by his pursuers shortly before the checkered flag.

He wanted to win and did everything for it. Next time, his effort might be successful. Nothing ventured, nothing gained. This motto is also true in business. If you have a business idea that will make money, you have to take risks. It starts with funding, very often by bank loans, or later, once the business is on its way, with finding employees. In between, you will be confronted by a lot of obstacles and risky decisions resulting from those obstacles which you will also have to cope with. Of course, particularly with risky changes, a corresponding improvement has to be in evidence clearly, but how often are you trying to effect such changes? Don't yield to stagnation in advance too often and thus resist changes!

Changes are your chance.
You just have to see them that way!

Successes make you feel good, but failures teach you a lot.

I dedicated ten years of my life to achieving my goal.

Together, we are strong.

I have realised my dreams.

Only what you do yourself counts.

Boot yourself out of your comfort zone.

Goals intoxicate.

Once you find yourself …

Motivation is the motor, concentration the turbo.

Think positive.

Concentrate on the essential.

THE ROADBLOCKS TO SUCCESS

In the course of my career, I celebrated a lot of wonderful victories. I won the Race Across America three times, set the world record in "Across Australia", won the XXAlps and some 24 hour races, and climbed Mt. Everest. For all this, I received a lot of cups and medals. But for my own private list, I would have to add to my house in Upper Austria to make room for all those cups. This is, because all my own triumphs and successes are not only those shiny cups I got in competitions but also those invisible ones I should have received for my successes as a father or business man. You can only enjoy success and happiness when you have pursued your dreams, visions and goals consistently and when you have realized them. I am proud of my daughter, who has meanwhile grown up into an independent young woman. Together with my wife I built a house in a beautiful spot, and my businesses, which are going to challenge me even more in the future, are doing well. I'm leading a fulfilling life, and I concentrate on things I can do and enjoy. To stick to your goals consistently is what matters most, if you want to be successful.

Even with roadblocks which bar your way,
you can build something good!

Many people are dissatisfied with their situation and constantly run after visions they are never going to reach, because they are often not properly defined, not pursued consistently enough, and unrealistic. How easy it is to hide behind excuses! If I had said on every rainy day, "I won't go out for training today, it is too wet!", I would have paid for such laziness at the next race. And who turns to excuses once will have even less restraints to give up the next time around! Excuses are also willingly used to protect oneself from other people, to push away the responsibility. I only have to recall the Race Across America of 1999. I started as the great favourite, and after almost 5,000 kilometres and 9 days riding time, I crossed the finishing line in second place, one foolish hour behind the winner. Just one hour? That's approximately as if a cycling pro were to win the Tour the France at the final sprint. My disappointment was correspondingly big. At the finish, I was busy exclusively with finding excuses and people to blame: the team was to blame, because once they sent me into the wrong direction; because a defect on the bike took too long to be fixed; because I wasn't given enough water in the Texas desert; because they had urged me to cross a red light and I was given a time penalty for that. The list of excuses got longer and longer. It was only months afterwards that I employed myself with the actual reasons for the failure and came to the conclusion that it was me and nobody else who had been responsible for it! I felt very sorry for having criticized my team members, who had supported me right across America in such an exemplary way. On the other hand, I am an extreme athlete, thus I have to have a certain degree of egoism. But victory at this RAAM had been a liability, sponsor money depended on it. Therefore, I felt pressurized and did not want to win but had to! Today I know that I must not look for a scapegoat but have to solve the problems myself. Transferred to 1999: I had been responsible for the failure myself. It had been me who had made the tactical considerations, who had decided on when to sleep, and it had been me who had put together the crew!

An excuse is the classical method to shift your own mistakes to others. So you don't have to criticize yourself. Or if you keep things away from you that you don't like doing. Roadblocks that bar your way are always an obstacle, but sometimes, you can also learn something from them. One of such educating obstacles I came up against in 2000. At that time, I had already decided to climb Mount Everest and was already deep in preparations. If you want to get up on the world's highest mountain, it's better to do a trial expedition before. But where to, and most of all, when? In 2000, my major goal was to celebrate my second triumph in my 5th participation in the Race Across America, after two second and one third place in the previous years. I decided to reconcile the two projects: for January 2000, I planned a mountaineering tour on the Aconcagua in South America, with its not quite 7,000 metres the highest mountain outside Asia, and my fifth start at the RAAM in mid-year. But the preconditions for climbing the Aconcagua were anything but ideal. Before my departure to

South America, I already fought a slight fever and a cold. My physician was worried and warned me that my problems would increase with increasing height. However, I would not be influenced by this, accepted the warnings with a good will, and set out. After my landing in Santiago de Chile, I caught my breath there for a few days to cure myself thoroughly. There was plenty of time to make the final preparations on location. With only a slight cold, and with four companions, I started the climb up the base camp in Playa del Mula at 4,300 metres. For a proper mountaineer, this would have been nothing but a banter not worth mentioning. For me, however, this trip turned into a seemingly insurmountable obstacle. With the greatest effort, I dragged myself towards the base camp, with each step, the dream of reaching the peak waned more and more. I suffered from weakness, short breath, ran a fever and had an irregular heartbeat – instead of the usual 35 beats a minute in resting state, I was up to incredible 120!

After a sleepless night, I really feared for my life. In the morning, my colleagues took me to the on-site physician at the base camp, and he diagnosed an altitude-triggered pulmonary edema! This illness is frequent among high altitude mountaineers and is caused by climbing up too fast. At such an altitude, the pulmonary edema can even be fatal! My Aconcagua adventure only lasted for 10 days, and those I spent in the base camp. I had to break up the expedition and was taken down into the valley on a mule in a six-hour journey. I learned a lot of lessons from this: Listen to the signals of your body! We each of us have to adhere to nature's laws when sheer survival is at stake. Today, if I have planned a six-hour training unit and cannot see it through for good reasons, I turn back. Don't overdo it at the expense of your health! There is one key word which is starting to dominate the business world: the burn out syndrome. This is an affliction of people who only live for their work, whose thoughts only turn around professional challenges; people who on going to bed and getting up only think about what has to be done next, what they did not manage to finish today. A burn-out is often underrated. Lots of people think, "Ah, this surely won't happen to me!" The person concerned very often does not realize the seriousness of the situation and can no longer escape from the trap of helplessness on their own. So, take care of yourself, your soul and your body, and don't always move on the brink of your performance! Plan enough free spaces for yourself, treat yourself to some relaxation!

You are born to be successful.
Nobody can keep you from it but yourself.

Back to 2000, back to my home country, where I immediately consulted my doctor after my return from South America. To his utter amazement, my first questions were not directed towards rehabilitation but towards whether I would be top fit again for the Race Across America a few months later, in June. He made me come back down to earth by saying, "First, you have to be 100% cured, then you can do things normally again. But you must be aware that you will have to start at zero!" My relief was huge, and I could go on aiming at the Mount Everest project. After a fortnight's break, I hopped onto the exercise bike again and started my training with a maximum force of 80 watt and 100 beats a minute. This is rather depressing for a top athlete. In previous years, I had boarded the plane to America with approx. 20,000 kilometers of training in my legs. In 2000, it was barely half. How did the race go? It was amazing, to be sure, both for me and for my physician: I not only won this RAAM, I won with a record lead of more than 23 hours – almost a whole day – over Danny Chew! I covered the 5,000 km route from the west to the east coast in 8 days, 10 hours and 19 minutes! I pondered over this performance explosion for a long time and had confirmation from experts in what I found: during the preparation phase, I had restored to my body what I had not granted it through the previous years – rest, regeneration, a break. The rest had had no ill effects on my body, on the contrary: less often is more, and thus, in 2000, the Race Across America turned out to be the race of my life.

Think positive!

How many problems accompany us day after day, week after week, month after month? And how many of them do we actually solve? Confess, it is easier to defer difficulties than to tackle them and discover their causes! There are numerous excuses and subterfuges to talk problems out of existence or at least no longer appear as the one to blame or as a loser. Many people spend their lives blaming a lot of things for their problems: difficult childhood, bad educational circumstances, current situation in the family, relatives, insecure times with terrorism everywhere, financial difficulties, wretched job or simply bad weather! Don't turn into a master quibbler. Impress upon yourself: everything you can realistically conceive can be realized in your life. Approach a new business idea with enthusiasm and optimism: "I'm going to do this in such and such a way, I want it to be like this!" If you hesitatingly and skeptically talk about how you might possibly, after a year, if you might have lost a few kilos and possibly managed to become a non-smoker, might want to do a marathon, your vis-á-vis will dissuade you from participating, "A marathon? The exertion! You're mad!"

An optimist's thinking can be as one-sided as a pessimist's.
The difference is, he leads a happier life.
Charlie Rivel

The classic example for the topic of "positive thinking" is the one with the glass of water that is half-full: take a glass and half fill it with water. There are now two ways to judge the amount of water: the glass is half-full or half-empty. The pessimists among ourselves will choose the second option – "I certainly won't get that job" – and he refrains from applying. The optimists among us opt for a half-full glass: "Nothing is lost yet. I'll try!" An optimist's vocabulary lacks words like "impossible" or "unsolvable". Join the side of the optimist and see the positive. Try to filter the hopeful, happy side out of each situation!

Be aware of your surroundings

How will I manage to make the leap from pessimist to optimist? You have to work on yourself and bear in mind that a positive outlook on life on its own is not the sole basis for steady success. But it does offer an excellent breeding ground for it! Moreover, happy and confident people go through life more easily, and in crucial situations, optimists also have that little ounce of luck on their side that is needed. Following the motto: Meet your success halfway! If you want to achieve something and busy yourself with that thought intensively, your gut instinct and your powers of observation will increase. Take a woman who wants to have a baby – she will increasingly note pregnant women in the streets, prams and babies. If you want to buy a super car, you'll almost exclusively find that brand on the roads! Be aware that all the things you adhere to are happening. If you think you won't make it, it will happen that way. You will meet people and create circumstances which will confirm your opinion, the opinion that you will not make it. On the other hand, of course also those things will happen that you believe in. Because you will shape your circumstances and the group of people around you in a way that will confirm that you are on the right track! Therefore, establish surroundings that inspire confidence and optimism!

One thing marks an optimist: the vocabulary. As opposed to people who only ever see the bad sides of everything, optimists do not use negative terms. Take phrases like "If only I could" or "I'll try it anyway, but ..." Such phrases and especially words like "if, but, try, attempt, not be able to" must vanish from your speech. Language is an expression of our feelings, those in turn rule our behaviour, our appearance and our gestures. Adopt your verbal expressions into your internal patterns of speech and delete negative suggestions that have settled in your subconscious. Then it will be much easier for you to build up self-confidence, a basic positive stance and the conviction that you are going to achieve a goal. There is no room for doubt, doubt is poison for the faith and a catalyst for failure!

And yes, I'm going to make it

When I am in a race, I know that my chances of victory are only over once a competitor is over the finishing line before me. Up to that moment, my chance is alive. In the Race Across America in 1999, I managed to make up ground in a way that's to be remembered. The race had started that year more or less without me. I soon was way back, found myself last with a 14 hour time difference. I had to fight the heat and the expulsion due to exceeding the waiting period, and I felt ill – and was ill, too. It would have been easy to give up during those fateful hours, to pack the bike into the attendant car. Nobody would have tried to persuade me otherwise, they all would have understood. The way I felt, the way circumstances were, it really seemed pointless to go on for even a single kilometer.

But no! I faced the situation and thought positive. I knew I would get over that period of weakness in the end, and that is exactly what happened. I started to make up ground in a big way and thus reached the top.

Positive thinking to me means finding something good in any situation, be it ever so hopeless. Even if things go badly, "something good will come of this!" Positive thinking pervades every day of my life. It might sound strange, even arrogant and egoistical, but "love yourself like nobody else!" I often hear other people say, "I hate myself!" How can you be expected to like other people if you can't get on with yourself, quarrel with yourself? Isn't it most important to be on the best terms with oneself? I therefore am of the opinion that whether you have good or not so good dealings with other people depends on your own character. One of the most important words in our vocabulary should be our own name. Your own name should have a very special place in your own manner of speech. It is me who has to cope with new tasks every day, me who is leading an aware and optimistic life. And thus I lie in bed every day, go through the day to come, gather positive energy and tell myself, "Wolfgang, get up! It's going to be a wonderful day!" It doesn't necessarily have to turn out the most wonderful of days, but chances are good that it will turn out a great day!

I will get everything I want.
And also everything I fear!

The difference between winners and losers

What is the difference between winners and losers, successful and unsuccessful people? Just trophies and entries in winners lists? That's not it! It's not always the winners who are first on the lists of results, I am convinced that the difference lies deeper: because it is the critical situations that differentiate the winners from the losers. The ones do not give up as easily as the others, they stick to their goals much longer. We all have our experiences from sports or our professional and private lives. If it starts to hurt, you have the options: get over the obstacle or sheer off in front of it and thus give up – say "No, thank you" or "Am I stupid?". If once things go badly, it's easy to clear out. The winner says, "Give up? Never. I'm going to make it, and afterwards, I will see whether it has been worth it or not!" Many a sporting career is stuck in its infancy, because the will to give everything for a goal is missing. Many a relationship fails because at the first difficulties, the ripcord is pulled. If you want to get on in your job, you have no choice but face the challenges in the company!

Successful people have a successful way of thinking

In sports, success can be easily measured: everything that can be timed by a stop-watch can be checked easily. And there are measuring tapes, referees, ... In business, measuring success is a trifle more difficult. Of course we all know the successful companies like Microsoft or Coca Cola. But there are many many more successful companies that are not constantly in the public eye. A company's success can be seen in its balance sheet. But those numbers are very subjective: one person is satisfied with the result, another would have expected more. Still more difficult it is to pin down success in the personal area: here you yourself define what is success and what is not! The term success is judged by each of us individually and often too critically. Let your personal success happen: I did this well. Here I was successful! If you place your bar of success too high, you are overtaxed, if you place it too low, you are underchallenged. So the happy medium is crucial! And never forget: successful people have a successful way of thinking!

Winners are not afraid of obstacles and mistakes!
They are simply prepared for them!

Another big difference between winners and losers is that the former get over losses much faster. The difference is that successful people get up again sooner and more often than less successful people. A loser thinks too passively, to fatefully. Unsuccessful people surrender for various reasons. They say:

That's not possible
This cannot be done
It's all meaningless
I'm going to make a fool of myself
I was wrong
I've always done it that way.

And what does a winner say? He is convinced that ...

... the public will be enthusiastic
... nothing is meaningless
... it can be done
... one ought to follow new paths
... he is selfconfident!

One thing is clear, no-one is born a master, winners are not born that way. They create their success themselves, work on it by achieving the goals they set themselves.

Above, I have mentioned that winners are faster in crossing the valley of failures. Such lows are especially important in man's life, to learn from them, to be able to get through the next wave trough with more strength. During the XXAlps, a race that goes across four alpine countries (Austria, Switzerland, Italy and France) and

2,130 km with an incredible difference in altitude of 53, 063 m, I suffered from bad seating problems. In my projects, problems with the posterior are daily routine, but these were different. Even today, two scars bear witness to the pains I had to go through even weeks after the race. The pain in my posterior became unbearable, I consulted with my attendants how to get out of this trough. Solution-oriented actions were called for, because giving up was no option for me. My bum was ceaselessly treated with ointments, I got homeopathic painkillers. We even followed an old hand's advice who told us that in former times, the cycling pros at the Tour de France had placed raw meat on the leather pads of the cycling pants! As time went by, we got a grasp on the problems, and slowly, things were looking up. All those pains never made me lose my train of thought, and in the end, I not only overcame my sufferings but also my opponents!

Victories yield more percentage (with a ? sign)
– but failures yield more lessons!

CONCENTRATION

I can still clearly remember my first Race Across America in 1996. There was, in Irvine, a suburb of Los Angeles, right in the midst of the American endurance stars, a 28 year old European who wanted to participate in the world's longest and toughest cycling race. I couldn't stop marveling at the presentation of the riders: I saw bikes that were so much lighter than mine and also so much more expensive. I admired my competitors' attendance vehicles, huge vans containing sheer luxury, showers and massage tables. And then the TV stations and journalists. One guy had a microphone stuck under his nose and answered with quick-witted statements, his right hand on the handle-bar, and casually posing his left, anointed leg on the front wheel. I was highly impressed and uneasy at the same time. How could I – who had the inferior bike and the smaller attendant crew including a minivan – hold my own against those stars? Even before the start of my first RAAM, I made one of the worst mistakes an athlete can make: I only concentrated on the others and thus was even more aware of my weaknesses. I took myself apart and confirmed a word of wisdom that also applies to normal life: when you yourself get weaker, the others grow stronger! In the case of my first Race Across America I was able to quickly smooth out on the bike those invented deficits and imagined disadvantages. In this premiere race, I came third and also set a new rookie record. Never before had a newcomer been so fast!

Three years later, I made a similar mistake at the Race Across America. I was on the road to victory, at least till up to 250 kilometres from the finish. Being in the lead, I gave away the triumph that felt so secure, because I started to busy myself more about my opponent than myself. I was constantly inquiring from the people in my attendant vehicle, "How far behind is Danny now? When will he come?" I had lost my badly needed concentration. By constantly asking and inquiring about my competitor, I literally begged for the situation of him overtaking me soon. Danny Chew noticed that I got slower and slower, stepped on it and got faster and faster. When he finally did overtake me, a weight lifted off my shoulders. My subconscious went "click", and from that moment, I was able to concentrate on the race again. Victory was beyond me, though, Chew was a ridiculous 72 minutes faster. So I did not win, but I gained a further experience: if you want to be successful, look ahead, not back! Concentrate on your strengths to the last moment! This is true for sports as well as other areas of life. If you have to do something, be 100% committed.

Concentration can be trained!

At the end of 2005, I got my helicopter license and thus made a long-standing wish come true. Especially in flying, concentration is of enormous importance. At the beginning of my flying lessons, I faced the big challenge of keeping the chopper stable in the air, but it kept swerving to right or left. So my flying instructor gave me some good advice: concentrate on where you want to fly to. The flight got steadier and more pleasant, and I got to my goal!

Stress and a hectic pace play a major role in our professional life and our spare time. Each of us is available constantly and everywhere via cell phone and e-mail, so problems with time management are the logical consequence. What should I do first? Should I eat first, call my partner afterwards, do the ironing after that and see what's on TV later on, or should I do all of this at once? Those who do many things at once, don't do them very well. Mistakes occur. You can only give 100% to a single task. If you talk on the phone while you drive, the risk of an accident increases, you lose your bearings more easily, and moreover, it is not polite towards the person on the other end of the line.

Stress and a hectic pace are concentration killers. Concentration is an important success factor to focus on goals and finally be able to implement them. As easy as it may sound: in the course of the day, take a few moments, sit down on a comfortable chair or sofa and focus on a point in your home. Focus on this item – a picture or a vase – and concentrate on it for a few minutes, visually and mentally. You will see how difficult this seemingly easy task is. Many people cannot let go, are always wired up. Too many thoughts – important and unimportant ones – race through their heads. I congratulate you if that concentration exercise works for you at the first go! This is an exercise that can only work in the here and now. Often, our thoughts are racing ahead or turned on the past. But life happens NOW.

Now impress upon yourself a positive thought, a goal you want to achieve, and focus on it. It doesn't have to be a big wish, you can also concentrate on small desires. For example, during an RAAM, I never asked myself how far I still had to go ("Oh dear, another five days!"), instead, I concentrated on cycling. Even if it is hard to do, I constantly try to focus on the present: I'm doing even circles on the pedal! My aerodynamic posture is perfect! I get enough pressure to the pedal! Small interim goals are very important to reach the next bigger ones.

The end is near ...

Every concentration has to end at some point. Every time a big project is close to conclusion or a well-earned holiday is approaching, an automatic reduction in productivity can be observed. I also experienced this performance reduction in all my eight starts in the Race Across America. Normally, the route covers 5,000 km from the west coast of the United States to the east coast. The route is marked by a start arc and a finish arc, and in between there are approx. 50 time measuring locations that record your time of passing through. But what few people know, in the Race Across America there is, 10 miles before the finish, a so-called Penalty Point, where you have to sit through possible time penalties. This is also were the final ranking list is written, which means that this is the official finish. The unofficial one follows ten miles later and is gone through in a sort of parade. In each of my participations, I only ever concentrated on this Penalty Point and not on the finishing line. Every time I asked my crew how far away the finish was, I automatically deducted 10 miles. My tension span held up to this prominent point. And every time I passed this, the same scenario unfolded until the finish: it was sheer hell! I dragged myself over the finishing line by the skin of my teeth. My head was empty, and my legs would no longer cooperate. Because I had suggested to my subconscious that those last miles were meaningless, the final ranking was already done!

I have experienced similar things when running. As long as I am motivated and focused, I feel able to tackle anything. But as soon as the feet start to ache and I feel every muscle, my concentration wanes, and all I would like to do is stop. Soccer or basketball are other good examples where you can observe how important that tension span is and what happens when players lose their concentration: a team is in the lead 3:0 till half-time. Victory seems certain, and the concentration fades. The so-far defeated team notices the weakness of the former leader, who is in a state of dissolution, and makes up goal after goal. Once concentration wanes, even a seemingly certain victory is in danger! Those who cannot keep up the tension span inevitably lose. One man who held up to the pressure despite the high expectations set in him, is an Austrian double Olympic champion in ski jumping. His coach opined prior to the all-deciding jump of his protege at the Olympic games in Torino in 2006, "He only has to get down what he can do!"

The nervousness could be seen on the athlete's face, but despite this pressure from media and public, his tension span held up. He landed his best jumps so far and became the Olympic champion!

Focusing upon oneself

In cycling, there is one remarkable phenomenon: a single cyclist is a few seconds in the lead a few kilometers from the finish. The question is: Will he make it, or is somebody going to catch up? Top cyclists who constantly turn round to make sure whether they will make it, very often do get caught up. This scenario can be seen everywhere. If, however, a cyclist only concentrates on himself and the finish, the chances are better. Gernot Totschnig only focused on himself in his historic stage victory of the Tour the France in the French Pyrenees in 2005. Looking straight ahead and with his mouth open, he passed all those thousands of spectators and focused on nothing but the finish. He did not care what happened beside or behind him. What mattered was his belief in his own strength. It is clear that watching one's competitors is relevant. But what is more relevant is focusing upon oneself. If a company only busies itself with its competitors and does not do its homework, it will fail in the end or at least never make any progress in growth. So if an athlete degrades himself to a spectator of his opponent, he will no longer be able to perform properly.

Motivation is the engine on your way to your goal.
Concentration is the turbo.

Think of the famous Shaolin monks. They are living proof of what can be done by focusing. These masters of concentration can do things thanks to their excellent physical constitution that mere mortals would not even dream of: their abdominal walls are completely unimpressed by sharp spear points, and their heads are used to bend iron poles. In such moments, the Shaolin monk does not allow any negative thoughts and concentrates all his energy in one point. He does not ponder where the nearest hospital is or how he will get to his hotel room later that night. His focus is on the here and now, on the task on hand!

Everything that is done, has to be done with focus – body and mind have to be one. And gear down a bit. Try to do less, consciously step on your life's brake from time to time – "de-speed"! Because concentration offers you a lot of advantages: people who live in the here and now shut out fear, restlessness and nervousness. You gain calmness, because nothing can divert and unsettle you! But if you lose your focus again, your viewpoint will shift – it is no longer you who is important but your surroundings, at the cost of your power and energy!

If you do anything being taxed and with intensity, you automatically get tired – physically and mentally. Taxing capacities is followed by a disruption of the biological equilibrium. What comes next is regeneration plus adaptation to a higher level of performance. In sports, this is known as supercompensation. So at the end there is an increased performance level. How do you feel, how does your body feel, when you return from a holiday, from some relaxation, back to normal life? You ought to be filled with power, feel esprit, be bursting with energy, simply utterly relaxed. People who complain after a holiday that they need a holiday from the holiday have done something wrong! As have those people who return to their desks and feel like they've never been gone at all. Those have not switched off correctly.

Switch off!

Switching off and relaxing are of grave importance in daily life. At school, lessons last 45 to 50 minutes, then there is a break, otherwise, concentration among the students would suffer. If you have one meeting after the other, it is essential that you let go in between. Either have a coffee break or go for a walk. If you cannot get away from the room, avoid discussing the topic of the meeting also during the breaks. Let your thoughts roam instead, dedicate yourself to easy tasks, read the paper, listen to music. If you get the chance to withdraw to your office, do so. Sit down comfortably, let yourself fall, close your eyes, lead yourself into a state of relaxation, away from stress, arguments, discussions. Simply switch off! Watch your breath, breathe deeply and slowly exhale. Afterwards, you will be free for new tasks again, ready for new meetings. You can also apply a ritual here in order to stay focused from one task to the next.

When the time comes where you could,
the time is over where you can!

Above, I told you of the tension span that always caved in during my participations in the Race Across America 10 miles before the finishing line. Don't underestimate that span, stay focused till the end of your meeting. As in a soccer game, there can be interesting turns of event in the last minutes that require your full attention. You can't go and say, "We have covered the most important points, now nothing else of interest is going to happen! Think of the example of the soccer match, where one team was in the lead 3:0. This match actually took place. It was in the Champions League final in 2005 when the FC Liverpool beat the AC Milan after a 0:3 deficit in penalty.

It will be a few years to my retirement, nonetheless I'm thinking about it. Time and time again you read in the paper about the retirement shock. People who have worked hard all their lives, whose lives were planned down to the last detail from morning to night for years and years, and suddenly they have to go into well-earned retirement – they often face a dilemma. Their rhythm has been muddled, they don't know what to do with the newly found time on their hands. We all should be able to cope with this situation. What would your reaction be if suddenly your life equilibrium were shifted? When the balance of tightening and lightning the load of the tension span would suddenly go haywire? Find your golden mean between not too much and not too little. Retirement to many people is similar to starting a new phase of life. After school, there might follow years of university studies, and after that at the latest, professional life begins. While you are working, it is already time to prepare for retirement. Find hobbies, things you are interested in and will have plenty of time for in your retirement!

Live in the here and now!

Imagine Formula 1 champion Fernando Alonso sitting in his racing car, spooling off his rounds in Monte Carlo and suddenly finding himself beside the track. What has happened? It was no engine failure, the reason for the drop out had simply been an error of concentration! In sports and business, focus is the main thing. A Formula 1 champion has to be highly focused almost every weekend during trial runs, trainings, qualifying and world championship races for hours on end. His concentration phase is laid down to the dot. When I do a Race Across America, my concentration phase also is laid down to the dot, but it lasts 100% longer: eight days or more. For such a length of time, it is extremely difficult, close to impossible, to be focused all the time. The definition of the term concentration is to focus one's thoughts over an extended period of time on a certain task, on the main thing, and in doing so curtain off other influences! This leads to the logical conclusion that you can only deal with the matter on hand in the here and now, in the present. Concentration cannot be forced and only works when you are calm and relaxed! For example: light a candle and watch the flame for so long until you have a picture of it in your mind. Then close your eyes and let the fire, the flame burn on in front of your mind's eye. Concentrate on it and visualize the light. Do this for a while and repeatedly.

My reply to the question what I tend to think about during an 8-day race is: very trivial things, mostly. With such an extremely long concentration phase, there are many possibilities for manipulation and distraction. Although I always try to keep my mind on what I'm doing – cycling – this does not always work. It happens that I am annoyed about the densely packed streets and the vehicles passing by so closely, or about the state of the race, an error of one of my crew members. Such external influences cost time and energy. If, with the same effort, I think of myself, my round pedaling, the next timing station, my aerodynamic posture, simply on the things I'm doing right then, I am certain to be going 2 or 3 km an hour faster. If I transfer this mathematics example to the Race Across America: with a racing distance of 4,800 kilometres and a journey time of not quite 9 days, the difference between focused and unfocused cycling can be a lot of hours!

Focus on the current moment. You can only do your work perfectly when you live in the present. It is said that successful managers distinguish themselves by only doing one thing at a given time and doing that thing with full focus on it. Thoughts that do not belong, like the next golf tournament or what to do on the weekend, are ignored.

To concentrate also means to be able to switch off. I compare this to a computer that is set to standby (a state of rest). If you are in the middle of a stressful situation, withdraw and switch off for a few minutes. Don't think of anything but yourself! This boosts your strength, you will see. We all know it is not easy. Because from our earliest childhood it has been implanted into us that we never must be idle, that there is always something to be done. So many of us are incapable of going into standby. But it is worth a try: if you do manage to really relax during a state of rest, the activity of your brain is also slowed down (this means that besides your physical activity, also your mental activity is reduced to a minimum). This state can be compared to "power napping", which describes a short but intensive nap during lunch break. You can tackle new tasks completely rested and relaxed. I used this technique for rest in all my projects.

Aren't there countless world champions in training, who always reach top times in trainings for the ski world cup but are never able to come up with the same performance in the races proper? Or take a tennis player who sweeps his better-placed competitors off the court by the dozen in training matches but who is put off completely in the center court by the pressure of the spectators and the background noises (applause, hisses, cheers) and doesn't hit a single ball. Many people cannot handle pressure. They start – and this brings me back to the beginning of this chapter – concentrating on others instead of their own performance. What follows is familiar by now: performance loss. Believe in your strength and do not allow others to grow strong on your weakness!

BE THE MASTER OF YOUR TIME

Statistics state that in Vienna, every second marriage ends up in the divorce court. Is there no love left on this planet? Or are we just a crowd of egoists only concerned about our own advantage? Do we live in a throwaway society where we get away with everything, where it has become too tedious to deal with problems? Do we simply say, "It doesn't interest me any longer" or "It has been a stressful relationship from the start, other mothers also have beautiful daughters!" ? Of course other mothers also have beautiful daughters, but do you seriously believe that a relationship with those daughters will be less stressful? There are discussions and quarrels in every kind of relationship. At work, there sometimes exist seemingly insurmountable obstacles. If you have a boss who thinks that he is the only one who can solve a problem, you will have a discussion with him if you can offer a better alternative. Problems have always been and will always be around, be it in the family, at work or in your private life. The only question is why all of a sudden we have stopped dealing with certain things: We don't have time anymore! Stress and the mad rush leave such a mark on our daily lives that we no longer differentiate between roadblocks at work or in our spare time. Instead of talking about them, discussing them, we simply push them aside! There are, for me, three clearly distinguishable areas, each of it with their own right to exist:

- **The job**
- **Private life/spare time**
- **The area of self**

All three factors have to harmonize, have to be harmonized. Nowadays, there is no balance between those three areas, unfortunately the job often is the dominant part. If you go to the playground with your children or chat to a friend in a cafe, this clearly belongs to the spare time area. Don't forget yourself, do things now and then that you enjoy. Go for a stroll, go window-shopping in the city, go to a cafe and read a newspaper. Create your personal spaces of freedom.

Do you know the feeling of waiting for somebody or of being stood up? Your sense of time is different and depends on the situation. If you are waiting for somebody, time simply does not want to pass. But for your colleague who is late, maybe because he is caught up in traffic, time seems to race by. When I'm out cycling for two hours, time goes by much faster compared to a half-hour training on the exercise bike. So always be punctual and don't steal anybody's time. I can still remember my training trips with

Peter Luttenberger. Even then, he was a determined young athlete who knew exactly what he wanted, who never took his training lightly. Once we had agreed on a time and meeting place, I couldn't dare be two minutes late. He wouldn't have waited for me and would have started on his own. I am an extremely punctual man and hardly ever late. If it should occur, it is an act of politeness to inform the other person of my delay. If I have a meeting and the other person is late – leaving aside really valid reasons like a broken down car – I see this as a slight of my person. If you have an important appointment, like a job interview, make sure you get there on time. Better to be 15 minutes early and walk up and down the corridor than to cause a bad first impression!

The quiet-time technique

The so-called area of self, meaning the time I spend with myself, is often rather ignored. Instead of staying home comfortably on Thursday evening reading a book after a hard day at work, one is again subject to social pressure; a birthday party here, a company dinner there. But each of us needs time for himself: to think about the day that has passed or the one that lies ahead. Let the highlights pass in front of you and enjoy the time. Simply spend time with yourself. Switch off your mobile phone and simply do nothing for a change! If you are constantly on the move, you will find out that switching off won't be easy at first. This technique of quiet time can also be applied to your private life. Tell yourself you will dedicate one evening of the week, starting at five pm, to your family, your wife, your children. This is our time, where job issues don't matter and must not be given room!

Does stress equal stress?

Stress does not care for profession or age: from construction worker to hairdresser, from primary school pupil to big business boss, everybody is "under stress" or "completely stressed out". But does stress equal stress? There is a difference between positive and negative stress. The majority of the people colloquially associates the word stress with negative things. This means your desk is disappearing beneath papers, the telephone is ringing incessantly, and you should be in two meetings at once. Or relatives have announced their visit, you ought to heat up the stove, and your children are in bed with fever. We all know days like these, and they put the question before us what to do first. Often we try to somehow reconcile it all simultaneously. We take on too many things at the same time, which results in lesser quality of the work. The outcome is what are meanwhile known as illnesses caused by civilization: stomach ulcers, high blood pressure, the burn-out syndrome, which is on the increase, and, in the worst case, a heart attack. On the other hand, there is positive stress, our internal driving power. It causes us to be creative and to work better. This kind of stress is essential, it expands your senses and keeps you alert!

It is not little time that we have,
it is a lot of time we do not make use of. Seneca

The critical question to ask if you find yourself in a stressful situation, is: How do you handle challenges? Do you feel pressurized in difficult situations, or do you see them as a challenge and come out strengthened? Depending on how you answer the question, you either fall back on old patterns of behaviour or you are able to mobilize new powers, find new solutions to step onto new paths. In exactly such situations, which demand your full attention, you can apply what you have learned and show your flexibility. If at work you have to go through heaps of files, return customer calls at the same time and rush from one meeting to the other, first do what you think is most important. Structure your tasks and deal with those who share similarities in one go. However, be aware of the priorities: the most urgent tasks are not always the most important ones.

If you set the priorities cleverly, you save yourself stress. A lot of time at work is spent in business discussions, so-called meetings, that are called about every topic, be it ever so trivial. In such meetings, what is discussed very often are the problems and hardly ever the solutions. These meetings have to be evaluated according to their priorities. If your boss wants to discuss a new project, you have to shine by being there. If your colleagues want to complain about others for hours on end, you can forget about that appointment. A lot of things are a question of priority, particularly important for an athlete's success. Top priority goes to training and regeneration. When I was still in a job and my career as an extreme athlete was only just beginning, my priorities were clear even then. By strict planning and dividing of my time, I managed to coordinate sports, family, my independence as a retailer, and my education.

Time management is an important topic for each of us. And not only starting from the day the leading time management expert Lothar Seiwert started selling millions of his books. I present the topic from my point of view, and my key statement is: Set your priorities, concentrate on one task at a time, and you will successfully finish it.

How to deal with stress?

The sensation of stress depends on a lot of factors. Even the way you feel from day to day plays a role. If you slept badly, you are more irritable. Thus some minor issue that normally would not have mattered at all can turn into a big catastrophe. A certain amount of tension – the positive stress – often is crucial to survival. In moments of danger, for example in an accident, a lot of adrenalin is produced. This hormone causes the body to react quickly and instinctively. Think of dangerous traffic situations. You are driving in a queue of traffic on the motorway, and suddenly the brake lights of the car in front of you flare up. As an instinctive matter of course you do what has to be done, you also step on the brake gently or hard, you switch on the hazard warning lights. These are situations where you don't have to think at all, must not think at all!

Aside from the negative and positive stress, there also exists the comfort stress. Think back on lovely times, lovely experiences. When you were in love the last time, or when your boss offered you compliments and a pay rise. At such moments, you're alert and completely focused. Your pulse rate is going up, your hands get sweaty and your knees start to shake. The same symptoms occur as with "real" stress. It differs from negative stress in that a situation can be felt as exhausting or pleasant. If the negative tension continues for too long, there comes a moment when you feel overtaxed, and you get stressed out. At such a moment you will hardly manage to switch off. On the contrary: in order to get this challenging situation out of the way as soon as possible, you invest more energy and thus fall into a vicious circle, where, fighting stress, new stress is created.

Say No!

Saying No is not disgraceful. There are too many yes-men anyway who let themselves be drawn into a stress-dominated maelstrom. How fast one can be caught in the negative spiral of stress is demonstrated by the following story: I knew a media-coach who only knew the word No from hear-say. He was at the beginning of his career and had to accept all commissions that were thrown on him. Soon, 24 hours a day were no longer sufficient. The maelstrom started spinning. Many customers made his life hell, each weekend was spent with work. Often, everybody wanted him at the same time, so he became a slave of the system. The continual disability to say No found an end in a burn-out syndrome and put the man out of action for months. Alan Lakein coined the sentence, "If you let time slip through your fingers, you let life slip through your fingers." How right he is! One of my first lectures in Germany led me to a company of world renown – Daimler Chrylser. There, I was talking to an elite audience, all the top managers of the company. The head of Human Resources amazed me after the lecture with a statement he directed to his employees, "In order to perform well, you have to be able to say No!"

Saying No will not always put you in other people's good books, but it will be good for your personality and your wellbeing. If you want to go on a one-hour run, go. And don't let yourself be distracted from it. Like your wife asking you to go shopping or take the children to the playground. Or your boss asking you to take on one more project, although you're already spending 13 hours a day in the office. Take the courage to say No. It's only two letters, and they can change your life. And there is a positive side-effect: one day your boss is going to accept your No!

Find your balance!

For your mental and physical health it is important to find a natural equilibrium between positive and negative stress on the one hand and a balance between tension and relaxation on the other. In nature or in our own lives, we can find many examples that depend upon each other for their existence: day – night, summer – winter, plus – minus. If you live under constant stress and cannot switch off any more, your body will one day be unable to keep up the pace. The worst outcome of this are the well-known illnesses caused by civilization. On the other hand, a life in utter relaxation is not to be recommended, either. Your body would lose all tension and vitality. The golden mean is the decisive factor!

In order to set up your own personal stress-fighting strategy, you first have to answer a few questions. Do the following statements sound familiar?

- **You work even harder to save time!**
- **You complain to your partner about the ever increasing burden!**
- **First, you light a cigarette!**
- **You try not to show that you are nervous!**
- **You take tranquilizers!**

All these are natural but short-lived solutions that lose their effectiveness with the next case of stress. People suffering from a lot of stress have to find out the natural triggers and cut them determinedly. External influences can be found in traffic, constant time pressure (you always have the urge to run after something), overtaxing at work. With such external stress factors, time usually is the main problem. If you are caught up in a traffic jam daily, why don't you switch over to public transport? Set yourself a time-limit in meetings: how long should the discussion last? Why don't you take time for your lunch instead of wolfing it down? If you are constantly late for work, why don't you get up 15 minutes earlier? It would be best if you observed yourself for a period of time and noted down each evening which stress situations you had been caught up in that day. This way, you will soon have a good overview of the triggers and can think about further steps to come to grips with your stress.

Apart from the external stress factors, there also are internal ones: fears of loss and failure, exaggerated feeling of responsibility, competitive thinking, etc. These factors are much harder to deal with than the external ones. It is too easy to blame the partner, the colleagues, the taxi driver or the boss! Admit to yourself that your stress is due to your perfectionism. The best recipe for facing such difficulties that are triggered by your own personality is to consciously relax (take time off for yourself, five minutes are enough), and reflect on your inner worth. You will soon note progress and feel generally better and more efficient.

Talking about efficiency – my personal advice how to best reduce stress is a lot of exercise out in the fresh air. I am not talking of extreme sports here. Lazy activities outside, balanced nutrition and enough sleep often do wonders!

CONCENTRATION EXERCISES

Even if you think all the following examples easy, they are suitable for old and young. The goal of these concentration and visualization exercises is to make you able to concentrate on a thing over a longer period of time.

1. Exercise: Secret writing

Decode the secret message!

N	E	O	L	I	H	R	A	D	W	T	V
5	7	2	4	6	12	1	9	10	11	8	3

4,6,3,7 6,5 8,12,7 12,7,1,7 9,5,10 5,2,11

______ ___ ______ _______ ______ ______

2. Exercise: Read the text

!uoy tnaw ti! uoy lliw ekam ti!" si a ylgnimees elpmis ecnetnes htiw a tol fo laitnetop. A laitnetop i tnaw ot nialpxe ni siht. i ma gnitirw ereh tuoba ym lanosrep secneirepxe dna ecitcarp i deniag gnirud ym efil sa na emertxe etelhta, ylimaf nam dna ruenerpertne. Ym cisab egassem si: gnihton skrow yb flesti.

3. Exercise: Read the text

Concentrate and try reading the text. You will see that without focusing, this isn't so easy. And try to read the following lines with increasing speed:

"YOUWANTIT?YOU'LLMAKEIT!"

SUCCESSFULPEOPLEDON'TJUSTFALLFROMTHESKY.THERE ISNOCLASSIFICATIONOFSUCCESSFULANDUNSUCCESSFUL. EVERYBODYHASTOWORKFORHIS/HEROWNSUCCESS, SOMETIMESONEHASTOFIGHTFORIT.OFTEN,ONEHASTO FACEDESTITUTION.TIMEANDTIMEAGAIN,ESPECIALLY AFTEREXTREMECYCLERACESWITHTHOUSANDSOF KILOMETERSANDAMINIMUMOFSLEEP,IWASCONFRONTED WITHCATCHWORDSLIKE"INHUMAN,ABNORMAL, INCREDIBLE,EXTREME".TOME,HOWEVER,MY8 PARTICIPATIONSINTHERACEACROSSAMERICAAND CROSSINGAUSTRALIA,CLIMBINGMOUNTEVEREST,ALL

THISWASN'TASUPERHUMANOREXTRATERRESTRIAL THINGTODO.INMYLIFE,IHAVECOVERED650,000 KILOMETRESONTHEBIKE,THISISEQUIVALENTTO15TIMES ROUNDTHEEARTH.MYPROFESSIONASATHLETEISNOW HISTORY,ANDIHAVEALWAYSSEENITASSOMETHINGNORM AL.INANYCASEMORENORMALTHANSITTINGBEHINDA DESKFOR8HOURSADAY.

4. Exercise: Spread Letters

Only using one finger, type the following sentence five times!

I always think positive

F L O B

U Q H J

A X G

T R W

M E P

Z I D Y

K C V S N

5. Exercise: with candle

Light a candle and gaze into the flame. Block out all other influences; think of nothing but this light. Focus on the flame.

Now close your eyes and let the candle continue to burn before your inner eye. Disregard all other thoughts. Concentrate all your thoughts on the candle!

FINDING GOALS

1. Exercise:

Take a sheet of paper and fill it with your goals.
Take your time, think about them thoroughly:

Note down your personal goals:

Short-term	Mid-term	Long-term

Note down your professional goals:

Short-term	Mid-term	Long-term

2. *Exercise:*

Well done! Now answer the following questions:

Why have I chosen these goals?
What has been the most important reason,
a special interest or faith in them, or the challenge?

Goal 1 ______________________________

____

Goal 2 ______________________________

____

Goal 3 ______________________________

____

Goal 4 ______________________________

____

Goal 5 ______________________________

____

3. Exercise:

How do I want to achieve these goals? What is the strategy behind them? Will I change my daily routine? Am I dedicatedly going to start looking for a job?

Goal 1 ______________________________

____

Goal 2 ______________________________

____

Goal 3 ______________________________

____

Goal 4 ______________________________

____

Goal 5 ______________________________

____

4. Exercise:

Visualize your goals and learn to live them! In order to visualize reaching your goals, just imagine what it will be like once you have achieved them:

You are planning to build a house? Imagine yourself sitting in front of the open fire, in the garden. What colour are the walls? What does your bedroom look like? What decoration will your guests see in the hall?

You want to lose weight? Imagine what you will look like. How you choose clothes of a smaller size in the shop, how your surroundings will change, how your friends will shower you with praise. Imagine how your sex-appeal goes up.

Only once you have internalized your goals and are able to visualize them, you are ready to change the mental attitude you need to achieve your goals successfully.

RELAXATION EXERCISES

1. Exercise: breathing exercises

Breath is life! People take between 10 and 18 breaths a minute. Breathing is therefore the most important life source. We can live a few days without food and water, but only a few minutes without taking breath. After three minutes sensitive brain cells die. The respiratory tract is the most sensitive part of your entire body, and the first to react to stress situations (through rapid breathing).

Conscious and thus correct breathing can not only heighten your physical wellbeing, but also stimulate your intellectual and spiritual powers. Moreover, deep breathing changes your mental state. You become calmer and more balanced. You now get your second wind. The act of taking breath re-activates all your life's forces.

Conscious breathing comprises three phases:

inhalation exhalation pause for taking breath

Use the calming effect of breathing not only in stressful situations: choose a peaceful spot, close your eyes, breathe slowly and deeply in and out. Take your time when exhaling. Begin for a few minutes, and repeat two or three times a day. Pay particular attention to your exhalation! When exhaling think consciously of your personal buzz words, such as Peace, Success, Health, Happiness, ... Another example: count your various breathing phases. Sit on a chair, close your eyes and relax. Breathe quite normally. Concentrate on your breathing. Count to yourself every completed exhalation and every impending inhalation: 1 for the first phase (inhalation plus exhalation), 2 for the next phase, and so on until 5; then begin again at 1. Count in your mind. Try to feel the air flowing in and out as you take breath. You will soon become aware that your reason, and the many imaginative thoughts it generates, tries to prevent you counting. Once you notice you are drifting, gently coax your reason back to the counting channel. Slowly return from the relaxation phase and open your eyes.

2. Exercise: Progressive Muscle Relaxation

Progressive muscle relaxation is a process whereby the physical act of muscle tensioning and relaxation is transferred to the mental and spiritual domain. The method is very simple; and therefore well suited to – and easily learnt by – each and every one of us. E. Jacobson developed this method in light of his finding that anxiety and mental stress in people always produce signs of physical tension. He further discovered that physical relaxation prevents not only such feelings as anxiety, nervousness and anger but also difficulties in concentrating. A state of relaxation therefore blocks these states and emotions. Jacobson now had the idea of generating states of physical relaxation and thus of eliminating its antithesis.

E. Jacobson originally developed his Progressive Muscle Relaxation Process in 16 parts. Being very time-consuming, it cannot be used every day. I therefore prefer the 7-part version, which is just as effective.

Ask your partner to read out the following exercise slowing and carefully; or purchase one of the many CD's. It takes a bit of getting used to – but with a little practice you will be fine.

Progressive muscle relaxation in 7 parts:

Find a comfortable posture. Check that everything is all right. For the following exercise you will need 10 – 12 minutes.
Closing one's eyes makes it easier to concentrate and helps to shut out distracting stimuli. So now close your eyes.

Be aware of yourself lying there.

If you want to be even more comfortable, you can loosen the muscles a little more, relax as much as possible. You will soon evenly tense certain muscle areas for 5 to 10 seconds and then let go completely for approx. 30 seconds. Please only increase the tension to a point where you can clearly feel it. Just up to a point where it feels good for you and does not hurt or cramp.

Now concentrate on your right arm.
Consciously realize how the arm feels.

Tension: tense as many muscles of your right arm as you can by making a fist, by bending the arm and thus tensing the forearm and the upper arm ...
Relaxing: now let go, relax the arm and your hands and simply let them rest. Can you feel the difference in your upper arm, the forearm, the hands and in each finger? Give yourself a little more time so the muscles can loosen up a bit more. Let go completely ...

Now be aware of your left arm.
What does it feel like right now?

Tension: tense as many muscles of your left arm as you can by making a fist, by bending the arm and thus tensing the forearm and the upper arm ...
Relaxing: now let go. Just let your arm lie there slack and loosened up. Can you feel the difference in the upper arm, the forearm, the hand, the fingers? Give yourself a little more time so the muscles can loosen up a bit more. Take your time.

Now attend to your shoulders.
Be aware of what that part of your body feels like.

Tension: raise up your shoulders as high as you can, towards the ears, and be aware of the feeling of tension in your shoulder muscles ...
Relaxing: now let go completely. The shoulders sink right back. So what kind of feeling is it now when you completely relax your shoulders? Feel and enjoy the pleasant sensation of the muscles' loosening and slackening ...

And on to the face.
What does your face feel like at this moment?

Tension: now tense up. Clench your teeth, screw up your eyes and tense up as many face muscles as possible by grimacing.
Relaxation: now completely loosen the tension. Feel and enjoy the face slackening and loosening up. Allow your face to become all slack and smooth. Feel what it's like at the forehead, the area

round the eyes, the cheeks, the area round your mouth – your mouth may open slightly.

Now please concentrate on your torso and your back.
What's the sensation here?

Now turn your attention on your abdominal muscles.
Be aware of the muscles,
of what this part of your body feels like.

Tension: tense your back muscles by moving the shoulder blades towards the spine, and at the same time tighten up your abdominal muscles. Feel the tension of the muscles in this part.
Relaxing: now let go of the tension completely. Be very slack. Allow your back and abdominal muscles to loosen up completely. Feel the pleasant sensation of the loosening and slackening of your back and abdominal muscles.

Now please attend to your right leg.
What does it feel like?

Tension: now tense the right part of your bottom and the muscles in your thigh, lower leg and foot. Stretch the tips of your toes towards your face and tighten up.
Relaxing: now let go completely. Your legs and feet automatically find a comfortable and slack position. Feel and enjoy the pleasant sensation of the slackening and loosening up of your bottom, thighs and lower legs and your feet. Give your muscles time to loosen even more. Let yourself go completely …

Now attend to your left leg and the left half of your bottom.
What does this part of your body feel like?
Send your awareness into that area.

Tension: now tense the left part of your bottom, your thigh, your lower leg and the foot of your left leg. Stretch the tips of your toes towards your face and tighten up. Be thoroughly aware of the tension. Feel the tension.
Relaxing: now let go completely. Let go of your bottom, the whole leg and foot. Loosen all the tension. Your legs and feet automatically find a comfortable and slack position. Feel and enjoy the pleasant sensation of the slackening and loosening up of your bottom, thighs and lower legs and your feet. Give your muscles time to loosen even more. Simply let go ...

Enjoy the relaxed feeling in your whole body.
You can feel the looseness inside.

You feel the ease with which the energy is flowing through your body. It is flowing through your legs, your feet, through your upper body, through your arms and into your head via your neck. You are completely relaxed from head to toe.

Now slowly tense your hands again.

Bend your arms, extend them and stretch comfortably.
Slowly open your eyes.
And slowly get up again.

3. Exercise: Positive Life View

Your thoughts are positive and optimistic. Repeat out loud these or similar maxims (of your own making) until your subconscious believes them:

I always think positive.
I will succeed.
I like working and love the discipline it brings.
I think positive in all situations.
I am strong and successful.
I can master every situation.
Today is my day !
...

1. *Exercise: the highlights of the day*

This table of highlights helps all those people who always see everything grey and bleak. Consciously be aware of the beautiful events of the day. What was great at work or at home? Did you see and enjoy a beautiful rainbow? Did you have dinner with a colleague? It's often the little things you no longer see. Note those down and make your own table of highlights!

You can download the table from my homepage
www.fasching.co.at/highlightsoftheday

Conclusion:

These are but a few examples of many possible exercises that can be performed. Further information is available on my website www.fasching.co.at. Further insights can be gained from my seminars and presentations.

THE WRITERS

Wolfgang Fasching ...

... was born on August 11, 1967 in Bad Radkersburg as one of four children, and he is living with his wife Doris in Neukirchen near Lambach in Upper Austria. He is the proud father of daughter Simone. Wolfgang Fasching started cycling at the age of 18, he was Styrian Champion and as one of the main cyclists competed for the national team; thus it was that at an early stage he already realized his passion for long-distance races. He participated in the Race Across America 8 times and won it 3 times. Every participation saw him on the podium. Beside his numerous victories – he was, among other things, 12-hour and 24-hour World and European Champion – he climbed Mount Everest in 2001, as the 13th Austrian to do so.

Wolfgang Fasching, who is a helicopter pilot as one of his hobbies, has written a number of books and is a much sought-after lecturer and leader of seminars; well-known companies and organizations in the German speaking world ask him to lecture on "Mental strength; set goals, achieve goals".

www.fasching.co.at

Martin Roseneder ...

... was born on October 19, 1976 in Waidhofen/Ybbs. Until the age of 19 he was a successful cyclist with the young talents, then he started his business studies. In 1999, he also began working as a journalist for daily papers and publishers in the economic field. Since 2003, he has been an independent PR consultant. Among his biggest customers there are, e.g., the Cycling World Championship 2006 in Salzburg, the ATP tournament 2007 in Kitzbühel, the Austrian tour 2004 to 2007, the Altstadtkriterium (historic city centre race) 2007 in Graz, etc.

Moreover, Martin Roseneder is the media adviser of top athletes like Olympic vice-champion Reinfried Herbst, the cycling professionals Bernhard Eisel, René Haselbacher, Peter Wrolich, Austria's top disabled athlete Thomas Geierspichler, and last but not least Wolfgang Fasching, whom he has been counselling since 2004.

martin.roseneder@sportpress.at

BIBLIOGRAPHY

„Erfolgsfaktor Kopf"
Wolfgang Fasching, Egon Theiner

„Du schaffst was Du willst"
Wolfgang Fasching

„Positive Unsicherheit – Erfolgswege in die Zukunft"
Werner Ringhofer, Alois Kogler

„Heute ist mein bester Tag"
Arthur Lassen

„Stress ade – Die besten Entspannungstechniken"
R. Geisselhart, C. Hofmann

„Spitze im Sport – Spitze im Beruf"
Richard F. Estermann

Meditations-CD 2001
Franz Steinberger, Wolfgang Fasching

www.erfolgsverkauf.at

Skripten Mental College Bregenz